THE SEA SLEEPS

New & Selected Poems

GREG MILLER

Greg Miller (signature)

THE SEA SLEEPS

New & Selected Poems

PARACLETE PRESS
BREWSTER, MASSACHUSETTS

2014 First printing
The Sea Sleeps: New and Selected Poems
Copyright © 2014 by David Gregory Miller
ISBN 978-1-61261-427-4

The Paraclete Press name and logo (dove on cross) is a trademark of
Paraclete Press, Inc.

Library of Congress Cataloging-in-Publication Data
Miller, Greg, 1957-
  [Poems. Selections]
  The sea sleeps : new and selected poems / Greg Miller.
    pages cm
    ISBN 978-1-61261-427-4
    I. Title.
  PS3563.I3787S43 2014
  811'.54—dc23   2014006321

10 9 8 7 6 5 4 3 2 1

Published by Paraclete Press
Brewster, Massachusetts
www.paracletepress.com
Printed in the United States of America

Contents

TRANSLATIONS

from WATCH (2009)

from RIB CAGE (2001)

from IRON WHEEL (1998)

Author's Preface

Song as much as smell sends me home and takes me new places. I was reared between places in LaRue County, Kentucky—both sides of my family moving north from the hills and hollows of Hart County ("Appalachia proper," according to the federal government) toward the Pennyrile's gentler, more fertile farmland and rolling hills, bounded in turn to the north and east by the Knobs of Nelson and Marion counties. My grandparents were dairy and tobacco farmers, and my father's father was elected for decades as county tax commissioner. My uncles were farmers, policemen, firemen, and factory workers; my aunts, cooks in schools, farmers, homemakers, and secretaries in the county courthouse. My father, a deacon, who for a while led the church choir, appraised real estate and then ran an appraisal company; and my mother began as a bookkeeper, and then became an accountant at Fort Knox.

I remember the Baptist hymns of South Fork Church near Buffalo, Kentucky, the Roman Catholic plainsong of Gethsemani Abbey near New Haven, and the Episcopal hymns of my young adulthood and after. Though the ancient, worn knobs of central Kentucky are a far cry from the younger, higher ranges of eastern Kentucky, I feel bounded by mountains. I have heard it said that Kentucky hills have an Elizabethan voice. Traveling with my father to appraise farms and homes that would give way to the new interstate highway system; playing with a boy who lived in a one-room house on stilts on the side of a hill in Pike County; hearing those musical voices, the long silences as well; watching old men come to the hollows to clog, dance, and sing: I'd say there was something to that, and something to my love, too, of British metrical forms that have their own indigenous American afterlife in the music of *Southern Harmony, The Kentucky Hymnal,* and shape-note music.

The African-American spirituals, the improvisational soul-lifting giving of the self utterly unabashed and total in ways unimaginable in white churches: I first heard that music at school. I felt a bit like the Chinese emperor before Marco Polo's painting: "Surely there is no such song!" Even today, when I am caught in a place without choral and congregational singing, I wither from thirst.

These poems come from an embodied form of the line, of voices moving over and within lines, sounds clashing and cavorting, resolving or remaining obstreperously, contrarily discordant. And my sensibility is rooted in a singing, fragrant place.

I have chosen to live in many places: central Tennessee; the Bay Area of Northern California; and for more than two decades, Jackson, Mississippi. I have lived in Provincetown, Massachusetts, on the tip of Cape Cod; in Cassis, on the Mediterranean Sea; and in the village of Marnay-sur-Seine, Champagne. I have tasted God's plenty, and I am grateful. I have a love of prospects, both temporal and physical, looking over what lies ahead and behind. These poems stand on prospects.

Yet place has no necessary or essential relation to poetic form. Patterned stanzas do not imply conservative politics, nor does free verse in itself necessarily bespeak freedom. Meters call to me, move through me, as does free verse: both are part of me, and at times the music moves between "formal" and "free." This movement between forms conveys a sense of my relationship with the divine.

When I was young, I thought my love of the natural world came from Wordsworth and the Romantic poets I studied in school, but as my parents and I talked, my father naming birds, my mother plants, love of our earth showed itself through my family. Our house was full of large, bright bird prints by the Kentucky artist Ray Harm. My father's father loved to fish, kept fancy chickens, and taught me to bark at squirrels in their own language. My mother's mother, like my mother, was a gardener: flowers and vegetables everywhere, even in old shoes or enameled pots and rusted wheelbarrows.

Yet, without the language of people, we could not be human. I have studied the French language and literature. In a Provençal town, buying dense bread with crackly crust, talking with an old man from the Maghreb as we wait for a bus, using the familiar, intimate "tu"— or "thou"—I once felt we were at home though neither of us was, nor was I blind to my privilege. Speaking, reading, and hearing another language makes me other than who I am and yet also makes me feel more myself. For these reasons, this collection includes translations of George Herbert's Latin and Guillaume Apollinaire's French. I find that Herbert's baroque makes the abstract visceral, while Apollinaire's sequence weaves strands of Christian imagery through pagan and humanist visions.

Devotional poems in a secular age sound strange, even abhorrent, to many ears. The world wars of the last century, and the religious wars of centuries before, left many of Europe's churches empty. Zealous belief too often fuels economic oppression and war. Zeal can crush the authentic human impulse. Without zeal's breath and blood and passion, though, what are we? The Hebrew prophets themselves declaim zealously against false religiosity. Prayer lifts the tent of the day, holds it at midday, and closes it at night. Faith in community, seeking God in the voice of another, is an ancient habit and song.

Two of my favorite poets, George Herbert and Emily Dickinson, struggled with themselves, their communities, their traditions, and their God. Their poems are full of conflict, with themselves and with their communities. Herbert could not have foreseen the dismantling of the Church whose corporate life was at the center of his poetry, though his poems inspired Crashaw, Traherne, Vaughan, and later humanists such as Elizabeth Bishop. He tends and extends a garden. Enraged "reprobate" saint Dickinson thirsted, her poems' yearning shining heightened life, walking the limits of language and meaning. Both, in their ways, are defiant poets of the Incarnation. God is flesh. The holy is human: the human is holy, here. God is in time with us, even in pain, though not in pain only, in the life of the body and of the mind and heart. The heart's fidelity comes first.

Many of my poems embody the intimate pain of estrangement and belonging. "It is better to be hated for what you are than to be loved for what you are not," André Gide wrote. But are those the only options?

A group of children from South Sudan, separated from their families or in some cases orphaned, once came to Saint Andrew's Episcopal Cathedral in Jackson, Mississippi. Their worship involved dance and call-and-response singing, often of the Psalms. I remember the young people dancing around a heavy nineteenth-century statue of the Archangel Gabriel standing on an orb, on his shoulders an open Bible. As the children jumped into the air, dancing, the heavy Victorian Archangel seemed to sway with them, too, in dance. Since then, I have traveled to South Sudan and visited their families and towns. Several of these poems also sing with them, the saints and martyrs, for healing and peace.

NEW POEMS

Primal

So I see now our primal people, pushed to the rivers
And coasts of Africa, bands of some five hundred
Individuals the evidence of our DNA strands now tells us,

The seeds of us all, winnowed and thinned by hunger
And thirst from drought, became omnivorous and skillful
At hunting and made tools for the hunt and, symbolical,

Made use of ochre and shells to paint and decorate
Our bodies, buried our dead with our tools and decorations,
Able now in life to feed the body's metabolic engines

With less but taken from more sources, shellfish
In due season, knowing the tides by the signs of the moon,
Planting and gathering and setting off together anew,

Great mammals falling extinct in our wake—the wooly
Mammoth discovered in upper New York State and painted
By Peale, lightning striking against the storm clouds coming—

Other humans and hominids extinct in our wake,
Little snippets of mitochondrial evidence
Indicating fathers in Europe inevitably my first father too,

And the other extinct sub-species—Indonesia's absorbed—
Like those of the Siberians and Chinese. All of this leaves me
Floating in seas of pre-history and indeterminacy like a bobber,

The lead sink and baited hook dangling down to catch
I don't know what, scion of makers and inveiglers,
Of the winners and the losers, of the lumbering

Neanderthals who left no art, who did not think it important
To leave prints of the outlines of their hands in dark
Caves, to set up altars with animal skulls, or to leave

God knows why the captured spirits of horses,
Rhinoceroses, and lions, flowing and to my eye
Holy as I see them now shimmering on screen

In a dark theater in an obscure small city without 3D
So I get a headache from the lack of focus and must lie down
Exhilarated still by my imagined companionable people,

The maker with the crooked little finger signing himself
Or herself over and over *I was here,* bones covered
Incorporated into stalagmites and flashing forth now

In the camera lights from the flickering projection screen
On the rounded surfaces of the Planetarium. The graphite-
Like blackened skulls of hominids I saw in display cases

In Nairobi's gleaming, multicolored museum, first
Threw me spinning down, the great jaw of one
Used, the sign said, to feed on nuts, taut muscles ascending

The rounded cranium. Maybe it's the simple
Insanity of our kind to make and then get on boats
Rowing towards a seemingly limitless void settling

Remote islands in the process, though surely many simply
Died in the trying, that's what gets my imagination going.
The petroglyphs by Sand Mountain in Nevada cover

Basalt boulders by a lake now just a dry lakebed surrounded
By mountains with rings left by the sinking and now extinct
Great Inland Sea. I climb Sand Mountain formed

By the winds sweeping sand from the seabed up
A thousand feet into the air and at the summit narrowly
Escape a dune buggy and Frank O'Hara's fate. No, it's

The folding over and into ourselves what we destroy and what
Destroys us that stays most with me. How we can
Stand side by side and look at a common object and decide

Together to act together, culture an accumulation
Of decisions, making tools that turn around and make us
Capable of anything. And the glimmering sense of purpose

And wonder, numinous depths, the great fish to catch
My bait? The butterfly prefers the artificial mate
To the reality it's presented. Anselm said it must be

True because it is impossible and we have imagined it.

Ruins

The city as a shifting ruin
Particularly though not exclusively
As an American phenomenon
Most of my lived life

Haunts me, blocks knocked
Down in "urban renewal" now blank,
Like Market Street in Louisville
Where Dad took me shopping

For fighting fish, whole blocks
Blasted, other neighborhoods choked
By highways: raised and roaring. My sister
When we were kids wore gloves

And I'd shine my shoes and clip ⟩ ✳
On my bow tie before the riots ∕
Left everything permanently
Different, Dad's car up on blocks

Once when we got back, his
Engine cut out, tires unbolted,
Leaving us to walk back to the office
And that's why, I think, we kept

Living in our small town, and why
Dad kept making that long commute.
I rode with him a couple of
Summers, working across from the Purina

Plant for Parks and Recreation in the stock
Room, some days the white powder
From the stacks next door drifting
In and making it hard to breathe

Or see. You don't have to see,
Really, the rotting heart
Of things much. The Gateway Rescue
Mission on Gallatin in Jackson,

Mississippi I pass on my way to Restoration Home.
Last time I went, on the way a woman ran out
At the red light and begged for money
And almost got herself killed by a speeder

In an old-model big American car bouncing
Over the potholes. Next to the Home
With its pillars and porch, a grand old dame
At one point, a brownstone with its windows

Boarded up; on the side street, a burnt-out
House still standing, roofless, down
The block from a purple church with iron
Bars on the windows called "The Temple"

And down the street another darker purple
Cinder-block building with a glittery
Billboard: "Danny's Gentleman's Club."
(The brownstone was my pastor's kindergarten

When she was little, and her daddy had
A store nearby, she told me.) This
Shifting I've heard called "creative
Destruction," the market's machinery

Destroying as it makes.
Somewhere in my memories of gloves
And bow ties there's the idea of opportunity,
Perhaps a genteel and vapid accoutrement

Of vanishing democratic false consciousness,
Where we might believe in a shared public
Sphere, where people might take care of one
Another enough for there to be a general hope

In the general good, that merit, not birth alone,
Might shape things, where everyone might have
A chance at work and dignity but
Now even Russia covets our Gilded Age,

Lit city grids at night like nets
Inevitably drawing us in and constricting,
But if freedom is anything
Really it must be other people,

Dear republic, dear cities,
Perishing and shining and shifting, though
Living can feel like a series of little strokes:
You lose yourself, you navigate the gaps.

My Cousin's Son

One of the first times I saw
My cousin's son he was a kid wearing
A baggy Canadian hockey jersey
Visiting his great-grandparents

(My grandparents) on their farm,
Down from Alaska for a visit,
And now he is dead. He grew
To be, like his dad, a big man

And I remember standing in
The front dining room surrounded
By my grandmother's doilies
And dozens of photos in gold-

Colored rectangular stamped frames
Of cousins, second-cousins, their
Children, their kith and kin,
Not always necessarily mine

By blood, and when we shifted
Around the room, the Korean
China my Uncle William brought back
From the war rattled in the corner

Cabinet. (When he was still
A boy Jeff shared with me
My brief boyhood propensity
To play with matches.) Jeff moved

With his mother, my cousin,
To West Virginia, though I
Think in his heart he must have
Always missed Alaska, where,

Quick, agile on the ice, he
Seemed to have been happy,
To hear him talk about it. When
Jeff lost his job, having a wife

Now and family, he stopped
His blood pressure medicine
Since he'd lost his insurance,
Still a young man, though no kid.

He died slowly. He wasn't
Able to get to a phone, and he clawed
The toilet seat off the toilet dying.
I want to take out a shot gun

And shoot whoever's on the other side
Of the door, whoever left?
Him there like that, I want to burn down
The house and everyone in it,

But the house in my mind must be
Metaphorical and this struck match
Burns me, my thought, my finger,
And I'm sitting in the dark

But not alone.

Lament for the Makers

I

Without rest, anger flavors everything,
And the sound of the titmice and chickadees
Tangling over seeds makes you cry

For the beauty, and your chest tightens,
Your head heavy and its horizon low, your teeth,
Even, hurting as leaden-headed sorrow

Carries you down: the boy's back beaten
Bloody, so as a man he kicks the dog
He loves, not knowing why, the dog loving

Nevertheless the hand that hits her
So she comes when she's called, crawling
Switch-backs, tail between legs, wagging.

II

The great-grandfather of my great-grandfather
Died on the Brandywine in the Mississippi:
"JIM FLOATED SOME FLAT HOOPS TO NEW ORLEANS

AND SOLD THEM FOR FOUR HUNDRED DOLLARS.
THERE WAS A ROBBER ON THE BOAT,
HE SIT FIRE TO THE BOAT, THERE WERE WOMEN

AND CHILDREN ABOARD. EVERYONE STARTED
JUMPING OVER BOARD ATTEBURY SAID
JIM WAS A EXCELLENT SWIMMER, BUT PEOPLE

GOT HOLD OF HIM TRYING TO SAVE THEMSELVES
AND JIM DROUND." An "Indian fighter"
Lies in the cemetery of the church that split

Over slavery, those against slavery expelled,
My slaveholding ancestors the remnants;
My grandmother with her long hair past her knees

Beside her grandfather, his beard to his knees,
Veteran of the Civil War though
No one cares to remember what side he fought for:

His granddaughter my grandmother
Took me to the graves of the makers:
The builder of a bridge in the West

Falling to his death in the making,
Then brought back to the Knobs—
These ancient, warn mountains—for burial.

A boy, I listen
To the Methodist preacher preaching
At graveside, he frightens me, I feel alive.

At home, I stand by my father at the blacksmith's.
I can see light through the slits in the walls
And feel heat from the furnace in the center

So I step outside in the chill October air
And can see across the misty flood plain
Where I think I hear the falls where the mill

First stood and Louis Philippe hid
So his assassins could not find him. Dad takes me to see
Sorghum cane crushed through ringers into a vat

Steaming rising from the churning
Liquid, the engine clattering and sputtering,
Men's voices rising competing happy to greet my father.

I taste and see the sweetness and dark
Bitterness runs together. They are part
Of one another, flowing slow liquid.

(My Great Uncle Chester in an old
Picture stands beside the Mill
He worked and owned, so twice a Miller.)

The love between my father
And mother undergirding me,
Sending me gently forth guarded,

In the storefront library I enter worlds,
I want for nothing, on the same block where Dad
Worked, a young man, in the slaughterhouse,

Lincoln's grandfather killed
In the corn and scalped, Great Uncle Lee's
House a mile down the road from there,

Halls, rooms, and basement full
Of clocks all ticking and chiming
And I stand a boy there in his magical machinery.

Meditation for July 14
Troyes, Musée des Beaux Arts

This Chatelaine's not
Masquing at Versailles. Her fair-haired
Children in red-gold brocade back her up,
Learning to accept gifts:
Two puppies slung in the shirt
Of a puppy of a boy.
The young are all learning.
Hierarchy seems a given
In matters human:
The deferential but not obsequious
Slightly downturned gazes
Of the family. To the right
A gratuitous colorful cock shoos
His spectral hens up
The ramp to the henhouse.
An old shepherd leans
Ponderously on his staff
From a near distance, the footman,
Ready to get on (it's dusk)
But not rushed, looking down on it all.
The comedy must play itself out.
The old man, seated, braces
A boy with his hand, as if to say
Stand up straight little man.
How easy to see
Only flattery and privilege, all the old
Ways to be swept away
Naturally, justly, we all know,
In the bloodletting that will soon follow.
Here's difference held in harmony:

Mutual forbearance, humility,
And something not unlike affection.
I want to believe what I see.

From George Herbert's *Memoriae Matris Sacrum*

What slight songs do I shape with my reed?
Mother, dewy with endless joys,
Tends, instead of a delicate garden,
An Eden no North Wind's blasts can pierce.
But as for me, the glory of my mother's name
And the things due to it are my heavens,
And while I watch over these things, the stars'
Ally often, I put off this creature flesh.
So rolling all my strength into my Sphere I
Press on tireless with my fingering:
Celebrating you, Mother, all day long,
By night, the light's rival, celebrating you.
Born into this world by you,
I am born into another by your example:
Twice you were mother to me
So your glory flies with twin flutes.

Air
(Juletta Thompson, 1909-2009)

Bright colors patterned and blocked
Mock my dark artistry
Less still than her stitched riches:
Purple pillowcases with tatted lips
And butterflies with the black-gold
Wings I'd see over myrtle as a boy;
The double wedding ring whose reds
Speak to one another through patterns
Of orange, aquamarine, and
Various wedged florals—waves
For outer edges—and then there's
Her sunburst's golds and yellows
King-sized carrying us safely
Again through night's eclipse.

When I studied in Paris she sent
A shirt with a rose stitched on the back
And ivy over the shoulders,
Buttons shiny white like ivory
That snapped. I wore that shirt
With pride though my friends rolled
Their eyes and shook their heads
And the professor made fun
Of my accent and so asked me
To translate into Russian, "the bees
Were buzzing in the wisteria."

After her death my mother sent
Back the carved wooden box
I'd bought for her mother with mowing
Money: umber oranges or nuts
Embossed on the top—and in it
The note I had written her.
Also: an envelope with seed,
A few dried flowers
From the rainbow Dahlia I'd given her
Five years earlier, with my name
And the date in her hand on the envelope.
(The seed would not sprout
That spring when I planted it.)

When I visited her dying in her room
Where my mother helped her stay
As she'd wanted to I told her
About the red maples I'd seen on my drive,
How her great-grandson had raked
The leaves in her yard. She laughed.
She shook her head. (What was the point?)
I told her I loved her, and she said,
"I know it. I know it," nodding assent,
Eyes closed. When my cousins
And aunts stood over her weeping,
Thinking she was at death's door,
She sat up shouting, "Give me air!"

From Fire by Fire

Mercifully, he woke up again
Calm; then he asked us lucidly
Was his bed set up yet at home,
So we had it set up. A man

Emerged from a van carrying
Woven steel: three pallets he slapped,
Chiming, together, clamped, to make
The bed where my father lay as he died,

His last long look a gift
So elemental it was like light
And water; it burns like the fire
That's spring water. It is as close

In this life as I'll get
To God's pure love; nor do
I fear death now: he is there first.
His diminished after-image,

I will give you, world, fading ash,
Not skin when the heart's rose is blown,
Not embers either, not dawn's glow
Through gray-fingered hills: spring water.

King David

The hospice letter tells
Us the family we
Should not be surprised if we
Fear we are losing our minds
Since three months now
Have passed since Father passed
And the whole world will think
We should have gotten over it
All by now and gotten back
To our routines though our lack,
Our love, lashes us
Binding us together racked
Miles away. At Eucharist
Even, I rock standing singing,
I quake and shiver and shine,
I fear, misty madman
That I am, low Sunday
After Pentecost, the choir
So few, I sit on the opposite
Side, not where I'm
Used to, and I see the boy
Over me in the window
King David, harp in hand:
"Sing to the Lord a new song."
My father was a David.
With my mother, he
Gave me his name.
He was a king of a man.
As a boy, he suffered so
The sorrows of want,
Madness in the household, remedies,

In ways, worse than the sorrows,
He told me once only
When I was a young man,
He always sought so to shield
Us all, but from this
He could not shield us
All tears wiped away
Where he sings now who
Was in youth a choirmaster
Where I ask, I pray, that his
Life song be for us a sling.
Take down Goliath Grief.

Father, Day

A father gets his son settled
In the train's rocking heartbeat
Hovering behind him to see
That he's all right.

In the store
I see caps that he wore
To please me—I'd given him one
He'd put it on to
Meet me at the airport gate.

As the procession passes
In this foreign church he sits
Beside me, he sees good here.

Through the crowd on the first
Sunny day in weeks, a Sunday,
A man picks his way.
Some unseeing someone
Kicks his cane, the man keeps his
Balance, he does not fall.
They hand him back his cane.
I stand for a moment beside him.

A bird peers engraved
From parchment. Will I
Buy him this? There's no
Wall space left.
In North Beach he didn't like
The bitterness of the coffee
I'm having. Before dawn
He got me up.

Even in my dreams he reaches
Through, he turns nothing,
I am asleep on the train.

Jack

Easter morning. A squirrel barks
High in the border ash,
A robin's robust new old song
Bold gold on a white sash

Of little snippets of twittering.
The oak fern's a black ball
Of unregenerate woven
Hairy tendrils so all

I have are two pots of onions
We crop when we eat beans.
Look: a mockingbird fans, rattling
Vents Pray tell what thunder means

In the distance that last night came
Inside, I dreamt, to walk
Chattering to its other self
(Jack Straw) up Dream's bean-stalk.

From that high pinnacle of woe
I saw tragic madness,
All of it, fall lamentably
Small, needless, and useless

(You reap what you sow). You can't see
Now can you, what you saw?
Balls of spiky spiderwort
Smother, lone green, my lawn.

I'd like to stay high so I see
And not be bound in a now
Whose no's no end—or ends bad—
Time's Theban, sad madhouse

To be caught red handed again
Not washed white with wealth's
Oblivion stolen but freely given
Goodness. The lyre sings and sings.

It's strung with the scheme of things.
I people my pockets with beans
Think June's sprinkler whispering
Yes. Yes. Yes.

The Begonia Bed

By my side door, red
On the undersides
Of heart-shaped leaves,

Amasses its phalanx
And turns silver
Towards the midday sun,

Edge to edge, each
Shield towards the one
Great Giver-Adversary,

To keep the moisture
In the cool earth
Under them all

So they can live
To shake their heads
Separately now yellow-green

In the good rain,
Dangling their tight
Double-chambered

Red blossom-beads
As if from strings
Under them to seed,

And thereby guard, gird
And extend the Kingdom.

Wanderer

I think I've found a path through heaths
though I can't call this dry rock, broom's
bloom, and rosemary's blue a heath.
The gray-white cliffs lift bony knobs:
"*the needle,*" "*finger of God,*" wind
blasting my face. I take another path,
still up, over the rise, until I see
Aleppo pines clinging to cliffs
across a gorge—then white rock islands—
and I don't kneel or fall but feel
like I might fall. Gold shoots through blue
so I see spots.
              I take switch-backs
down the cliff's edge back.
                     I grab at roots.

Before I reach the first *calanque*, its white
rock-sheltered beach, down a path between
two hills, I hear, after I stop, this singing:
serins and chats, and then, like hummingbirds
in pine cones—golden finches hovering
to feed, pollen-gilded—their cries like bells.

Portal

If you hold me here in your hand now I wonder
Do I cast a glow from your palm
Illumining your face, your feet kicked up in the waiting area?

I see your face shine peach-yellow though you
Can't see yourself as I see you or others see you
But I hereby exercise due diligence:
                                                    I warn you
I am no respecter of persons, I look shamelessly

Into private faces and I commune
Therein when I ought not to, I must admit to you,
And am frequently lifted and thrown in a blanket

Of chatter—my loud, garrulous countrymen—
Do you hear yourselves shouting, hungry to fill
The last, least possible corner of quiet, I wonder?

The waves of speaking, the querulous, the quarreling
Fed too by invisible interlocutors
And their instruments, louder for the absences
They must breach and the presences they must block,
These eddies and counter-currents and shifting

Lead lines of the song, too, part of the singing
I share with you as you hold me maybe
Touching me with your finger tips or as you spit
And you catch and turn

The leaves when you have finished
With what's in front of you. Or you

Have put me down by now. Maybe by now
Reader, I am rather the dust that flies dry
Into your lungs in the archives and this voice

Comes to you through the most profound
Stillness before I make you cough
Or maybe you've found me dry rotting
In a box in some abandoned cabin.
You have found me. I am well aware of my mortality.

Are you blasted too by the heat of people passing
(I admit to you I am sometimes close
To jumping out of my skin, the heat is so hot)
The gaggle of young women giggling ascending
Oblivious to everyone and everything pushed

In their wake, the young couple,
The husband standing and helping an old man
To his seat, the grandmother eating her eggroll
From Fancy Wok, ripping with her teeth
The packet of sweet plum sauce, the young mother
Nursing, covering herself with her small square throw?

I am a voice like any other and like you
I do not observe as I ought to the proprieties
And you don't know me at all,
And I am at one with you and you with me.
Perhaps we tweet together in the Empyrium
Of archived energies and we will meet there again.

You may take me into the woods if you like
And have your way with me or cut me up
After a while in the remainder bin even
And I will be none the worse for the wear and tear.

Or I will make good pulp for the last newspapers,
Or maybe my energy will be recycled
To travel the woof and warp of weaving speech
Or I will just flare out uselessly
Or you have stuffed me in your carry-on
Or coat or shirt pocket, you will carry me, you will take me
Past the expanses of intergalactic space,
Home, since we're formed of the dust of the stars.

"The Separation of Light from Darkness"
(for Dr. Rafael J. Tamargo)

The surgeon who will save her sight
Was first to discern
This creation: in Michelangelo's chapel

Nested in God's neck beneath
His chin's beard
Echoing clouds

Swirling like God's red robes
Turning diagonally, a screw
Between the light and the dark,

The light brightest above the head's bit
Cutting upwards towards light
Into which we fall,

Heads back, like His, as He looks up
And we look up at him:
In God's throat:

A brain: optic chiasm, cerebellum,
And spinal column all
Funneling down

The larynx that, conceiving,
Having spoken light, speaks
Now the separation of the light

From darkness, matter
Conceiving and
Speaking, seeing fit to make

Humankind in His image
(Michelangelo by candlelight at night
Studying life's secret lineaments),

The growth on the optic nerve
Threatening with its pressure
Intuited by the same surgeon, his *techne*,

Art, and experience, before his knife
Even enters the temple
To leave the young mother

Immediately after the post-op
Drugs wear off
Seeing more,

The drill of the dark, the twining
Excrescence of cells,
With his hands loosened and lifted,

Healing, through whom creation's
Transfigurations turn
Burning with a light not its own:

Art's throne and home. Healing
Come down is homely, too (my
Aunt May seized Doctor Gray

In her fierce bear hug
When he mended my mother's
Heart) and so too we

Here seize you.

Grounds

Saint John in his box broke through to you
Better, I'd bet, than his tormenters would
And that cracked half-breed Teresa's value
To you I'd reckon sweeter than wormwood
Though it's only spirits' flowers I smell
Now centuries ahead, since the deeds done
Against them pressed them (the church, earth's hell):
Redolent oils, fresh banks, near new Jordan.
I'd call on you, if I could, but I can't
Meet you anywhere other than prayer
Whose cool springs and nights water my inner
Desert and hot heart better than rant, cant,
Or calm alone, where a sinner might dare
Plead for this piece of work and love bloom better.

Missing: Refugees

1
One Returns to South Sudan

They slaughtered bulls and danced for days,
I hear. They welcomed you, and you are home.
You won't call me anymore to come with you
To court, to visit you, to find you food,
Or bring you doughnuts in the hospital. You won't
Need me to come take you to the halfway house
I helped you find, all of whose rules you hate.
I won't take you to church. You won't need clothes
From me, you're good now, you're happier home.

2
One Moves to Fargo

A doctor in a headscarf treated your ears,
Greeting the priest and me, the three of us:
"So who are you to him?" "These are my *friends*."
The hoodlums in your complex didn't kill you.
You won't pick fights with them, nor they with you.
Relatives in far Fargo came for you
At the station, and the train I put you on
Was a straight shot (except for Chicago),
And after the layover, you got back on.
You called to tell me the people there are good.
A year later in an email someone said
This winter you nearly froze, stalled in a blizzard.

3
Another to Chicago

You walk the streets and talk to no one there.
"My teachers loved me. They were all so good."
Shuttling by bus from city to city,
Leaving whenever you sense that you'll be put
Away again, bright light of a boy, still
Beaming and brilliant, good angels guard you.
But when the Devil spoke to you through TVs,
Computer monitors, everything wired,
It was all garbage and had to be tossed.
The medicines they gave you were all poison.
You have a place. You're good. And you still walk.

4

The boys all men, nothing I did enough,
Nor anything any of the many did,
What will I do, with nothing I can do,
Diminished, in their absent presences,
Aching to make for them space, and joy?
I feel an empty nest, like the one Mother
Went to outside her bedroom window, where
She saw one fledgling perched, all the rest flown.
She kept the cats inside. I can't do that.

The Burning of Lierpiou

That Pentecost, the "wind of the Holy Spirit" set fire
To Dinka land, the Dinka bishop tells young refugees
Around the dinner table, after dinner at the Bishop's,
And the people came to Christ. They killed their gods.

And the people who came to the burning saw gods jump
And scream (they did not want to die), but the god
Lierpiou everyone saw jump from the fire and flee.
It was night, and he flew to the bush. He stopped

Over the Nile in Bar al Gazaal, where he found
A magician, but Christ pursued him, and the children
Of this Magician became Christians, learning Christian
Hymns, so when the god told him to kill his children,

So that he might be powerful, the children sang
Hymns to Christ, their father could not kill them,
And the town chased the god away. He flew north
And still uses his magical lies and deceives the people.

The people burned their old gods, even the household
Gods they could hold in their hands, in the great fire.
The god Lierpiou, whom even the Arabs feared,
The god of the spear, had not saved them from soldiers,

The Antonov helicopters, the bombs, or the fire raining
While everyone fled, scattering, in every direction
Till they became themselves like little tongues of fire
And the great wind came spreading them everywhere.

Forgiveness

The young priest
in the Khartoum camps
          buried so many
  with his own hands

      that for a while he was driven mad.

He has come
          to teach the priests
                    to make their hearts clean.

"You must forgive.
                    Christ
From the cross forgave. Saint Stephen
      as he was being stoned to death

Forgave. You must do this
      not only because it is right
but in order to be well.

                    My torturer
                              did not know me,
cannot know God,—
                    he acted in ignorance.
                              I *forgive* him."—

(In the hospital,
                    visiting after an operation,
I see a tree
          on Jacob's back.

                              He has come
so he can hear again,
                    for surgery on his inner ear—
I see on his back
                    the thick cicatrices
                                        like a tree.
I have to see *him*,
                    I think, and not
          let him see that I see.)

                              +

Bishop Loyo
                    moved
                              through the forest

from place to place
                    so his pupils would not be killed.

"My ancestors
          saw God in the big tree.
He lived for them
                    in the heart of the forest
from which he would appear
                              to be with them."

                              +

     "The reptilian
                    root of the brain
repeats over and over
                    obsessively
seeking to be free

of the pain of humanity—
        the adrenaline rush, whatever the source—
            and we
    must use our frontal lobes
                REASON and IMAGINATION
                to see
a *human* way.

            You must forgive yourselves.

        You are
                angry
                        with God.

You must forgive":

        (Stoicism,

                madness,

                                the infant's
return to the womb—
            just about anything
            else makes more sense.)

                        +

He came
so he could hear again,
                for surgery on his inner ear—
I saw on his back
                the thick cicatrices
                            like a tree.
I had to see *him.*

                              Thanksgiving. Like sun
                              drying
phlegm:
              suddenly, lungs
                                   breathe
                                          strange joy.

.

                         I can't hear clearly what's being said.

                         I could break open.

Concert to Mary, *La Sainte Chapelle*
(after a mission to South Sudan during a time of war)

Mary, Mother of God, I would sing to you.
My heart is in the mud. Black flies and parasites
Make eyes milky and put out the light
Here and there one eye and sometimes both
Though at night overhead the constellations
Near the equator are no stars I know except
Perhaps a dipper low near the horizon
Milky light surging and dripping as we sit
Under the tree and talk and laugh, Mary
Mother of Milk, of goodness, pray for us

I would say, if I could, as the voices rise to cry
For us, earth's children, in this jewel box
Of leaded blue and red, the string quintet
Rocking and lifting me up like the baby I lifted
To still her crying since she was tired and fussy
And wanted this for a bit before she was put down
For the night, to be rocked, to be in motion
In the arms of someone whose smell she knows
In sight of Mother, whom she smells, whose milk
Is good, and the soprano looks at me and sings
Into me, I think, and feeds me and I am hungry

Oh she must think me a fool and a sentimental
Silly to weep so, to be pushed to this, but I sing
Too, despite myself, no I sing with you, Mary
Whose nature is song always, you, oh sweet song,
My lullaby, but no, sleep is a long way away yet
In the world for the blind woman who holds
A hand to her head crying hallelujah for healing

Falling smaller into herself and weeping silently
Or the old soldier, who's lost a leg and walks with crutches
In uniform on the road, still in service, with great dignity,
With the solemnity of a general, protect them, song,
Star of the Night, Star of the Sea, Star of the blank air.

Lesson

When I write to Mother
From my window I see
Down from my third-floor room
One tree in white bloom,
Evergreens, willows,
Blue wildflowers and graves
In a churchyard
In Wales, she says to me
This is good, this will
Teach you. You
Have to slow down.

Service

"Sir, I pray deliver this little book to my dear brother, Farrer, and tell him, he shall find in it a picture of the many spiritual conflicts that have passed betwixt my God and my soul, before I could subject mine to the will of Jesus, my master, in whose service I have now found perfect freedom."
—George Herbert 1633

"In whose service
I have now found perfect freedom,"
He wrote after
His Master
Wrestled for a heart and blesses
Ladders to a Kingdom

A lesser heart might
Stumbling, find, and, finding, lift
His mute despair
To a high chair
Of sorrow and dirt (a child's right)
Where heart-cries cross a drift,

Pilgrim's burden
Falls, heaviness in the chest,
Things left undone,
Still to be done,
Fear cast out, and tasks lighten,
Steps quicken, and there's rest

To be had I lose in my rush
To claim
My aim—
I mean myself—caught in ambush—
Forfeited—shot—with the gain:
I have to taste again
My Sovereign's pain and reign.

First Words

Though empty
(Don't tempt me!)
Ironic
Skeltonic
These bones rise
In surprise
To confess
They fear less
And trust more
Than before.

In the Pocket

"Thought of intimating that the Atonement was'nt needed for such
atomies!"
—Emily Dickinson

What if they're right? No God. And then no heaven,
Everything happening by happenstance
Alone. We'll say we're all, then, even Steven,
Our slates all clean, no calling to remembrance.
I do feel, really, more thinned lineaments
And figments twining after one Big Bang,
The great wind-down; I glow: thin filaments.
And entropy, what the Fat Lady sang
On her hung moon, though, oh, like a warbler
(So trite, so true) she tickles me to my toes
With her goodness, what she intuits abler
Than the night's Blank Queen she is: she shows.
She flows. This is serious business, this
Bargain basement sale: God's "thrifty purchases."

Corpus Christi
(chapel of Gladstone Library, Wales, 2012)

The chapel swept and cleaned (dear whited idol)
Roof-ribbing Canterbury's echoing lines,
Rubies and pearls, jewel box: here's a riddle
If ever there was one. Who's who? What shines

Here: Hearts, Faces? Who puts who through what paces
To what end? Together do we process,
Stumble, mumbling "bastard!" in holy places,
Vast inland seas (my lot, I must confess).

I need a better ship, fresh rigged. A jet
Would be better, still, giving, as it shifts
Headlong through sheers or turbulence, dead set,
Indomitably on: Love, being known, though, lifts

Me from myself, good company, holds: showing
God living is a different kind of going.

Laughter

Like a doorway between
The earth and sky,
The King, I think, is here, unseen:
Laughter and light reply
Where young men, fighting, eat
In the hot room
Upstairs and women who meet and greet,
Serving, are served. For whom

I wonder does this thin
Space fall a veil
Through which to glimpse again
Grace tucking his shirttail?—
As when, once, one singer
Glowered daggers at
Another from the high altar,
Stumbling, and all fell flat,

I heard what to me seemed
To say I was
Mistaken in taking redeemed
Concord for heaven's bees' buzz
And not true harmony.
Though dissonance hisses
Fights may just as well as any
Means show us what bliss is.

Singing Schütz

We fall up a weightless helix,
Pass links from strand to strand.
The Master's interlocking tricks
Quietly insistently land

Us higher, and more tightly bound
Inevitably up
Though down each time we take new ground,
Unworthy to sprinkle with hyssop

His ankles or to loosen the laces
Of his sandals, singing
After him as each part races
To fall, resolved, before the King

Still ringing though the singing stops
Sounding down the chancel
Less now than where the Master crops
Flight, stops, and bears away the bell.

The Sculptor and His Muse
(Rodin 1894)

The lithe muse rises from his crotch,
right finger and delicate thumb
poised where I watch
her rise
from his shaft's hidden head,
her left foot rising from his thigh
as from a bath
falling counter-clockwise
head-to-head, their shared wreathe-like hair
like Venus shed
or cut from Zeus to be thrown free

until the spinning lines make me see
her large left hand is his also,
she his shoulder
shock-stopped
by that face—east finished,
blinded and turned inward—
those pert small breasts
the clock's top, where he's dropped:
that giant right hand that's covered
the beard—the mouth—
vomiting and making. What lifts

his muse from the stone scrotal sack
or earth-womb opening between
his knees—earth-wounded—wracked by lack
and surfeit, stone lactary-sheen?

Day Tripper

I got up a little too late and took
The bike as fast as I could along the canal
Only to get to the train just before it pulled out,
No ticket in hand and the agent occupied.
As it turns out, there was another train within the hour
So I got to the Troyes station minutes after
The car rental place opened its doors and I picked up
My little black *Passat*. I enjoyed the crew.
The woman's short hair was spiked and she wasn't
Unfriendly, really. The young guy who walked me down
Wore clothes that fit him well, and he smiled a good deal
(Unusual here), nor was he "simple" like the smiling face
On the sign over the seats reserved for the handicapped.
The road to Dijon passed through several towns,
Up and down hills, few vineyards in that part of Burgundy.
The stations I picked up were *Nostalgie* and *France Culture*
And so I listened to a discussion of "auto-fiction"
By a young gay man who died of AIDS in the 90s.

He wanted to construct his identity out of desire
And transgression, a refusal to lean on outside
Rules to govern his choices or consciousness, and in this
He felt to me not all that different from many others.
I felt as if listening to a West Coast station
Decades ago, it all felt so familiar, except
I was on the road to Dijon to see Flemish paintings
In the Ducal Palace, driving through small towns
Whose narrow, circuitous roads made for slow going.

I visited a crypt in Dijon from the ninth century and felt cleansed
By the cool, the light, and the efficient symmetry,

Griffins, I think, clasping a man's legs on a capital,
Lifting him in their beaks and fantastical curled snouts,
Though it was hard, from the ground, to make out.

The dead writer on the radio had had enough
Of narrow roads, penitence, his father's shame, the old
Approaches of identity, his "self-fiction," even, transgressing
The limits of events but keeping them, too, transgressively;
I don't know, though, that we can ever really step out of the frame
Or that sex can serve as the sacramental solvent of old forms
Though I know some think still this is possible.
An older would-be mentor told me so
Years ago: what he thought I should know:
That the core of who I was, my self's best well,
Lay in an endless democratic giving
And taking, renewing in clear flowing
But that wasn't really me, nor did I want it to be.

On the drive back I could only catch "Nostalgie"
And so the sixties took me back to Troyes
Where, though my train was cancelled, I caught another,
Trying to eat a chicken curry sandwich quickly and without
Calling attention to myself (that's just not done),
Two teenage boys kissing extravagantly on the bench
Behind me. There was light enough to bike when I got back.

It's the gritty humanity of the Flemish paintings
That get to me and that moved me again when
I finally found my way after getting lost on foot
In Dijon. The face of Saint Jerome could be that guy
Who handed me the keys to the *Passat* and said
So long, I'll see you again this evening, good-bye,
Though penance shouldn't be for being me,
Or you, or a shadow, but self-sufficiency

And realism, if anything, here eschews embellishment
So that brightly colored clothes, buildings, or atmosphere,
The glossy surfaces make the faces and forms stand out
More than they might otherwise,
Flowing like light at night from a window or a face
And I think this must be part of an art that feels
Art's part less than the least of love's mercies
Saying (to me) leave all false penalties and remedies.

The Devil Whipping his Wife
(Self-Portrait at 55)

My back begins to bend. I am a Jaggers:
They rigged my spine with steel to drive it straight;
Four decades since of slumping-forwards weight
Threaten a hump-back; my ill temper augurs
The Thompsons' passions flying like a gate
To let good cattle out and pasture hate.
(Am I the little man I see who staggers
To the mirror, as if that were what matters?)
Mysterious Browns, who all died young, who
Were you? (Well, I'll die, too.) A purple heart
And a flag in a box with a clipping: may God bless you.
Millers, in your own vapors, a world apart,
Unknowing cloud. Composite of components,
Less than the least: lightning, sun, and torrents.

Rescue
(for Don)

You've taught me how joy's free and joy's free choice
Can open wide into the day
Night keeps close opening its display
Of what's to touch and hold. We are time's toys
And tops, perhaps, but those whipped and cranked old joys
Some boys pick from the box, we put away
For good and make our different kinds of play.
I rejoice and rock in the boat of your voice,
Your ways' weather and our days together
Not Venus on her shifting waves as much
As that Greek King (your motives better)
Who freed Philoctetes and took his crutch
From the island agony where he sat
Though his wound wept and he raged to leave all that.

The Garden of Earthly Delights

Phillip II, before he abdicated, becoming a monastic, acquired
The Garden of Earthly Delights, and was said to have displayed the triptych
Beside his alembics, his glass cylinders, for distilling the *Elixir of Life,*

And someone since made of the outlandish laughter I hear when I see it
A proper *Last Judgment,* complete with the harpist crucified
In his harp (the Spaniard making it all quite seriously dreadful).

But I've been reading Rabelais's *Gargantua* and *Pantagruel.* Epistemon
(Whose name means knowing) has come back from Hell and seen
The tyrants reduced to menial labor, Great Xerxes a crier of green sauce

And so I laugh at the "Tree Man" on the right, who turns to look at us
With what may be the face of Bosch (who knows?) as musicians
Play out his cracked butt, not looking in the least perturbed at their
    whereabouts,

Even the people being pooped by odd creatures with beaks down
Glass beakers to fall down the hole into which a drunken man vomits
And someone else excretes pearls; it's all so absurd,

But it's nothing like the central panel, an orgy of silliness, naked troupes
Lifting giant strawberries and cherries, supposedly emblems of pride,
I'm told (but who is to say how fruits signify in such strange terrain?),

Couples, trios, or gatherings fondling one another without scruples
Or contexts, one guy's rear poking out of a floating broken egg
As another guy gropes some slender woman's privates, and their cracked

Egg floats merrily along who knows where or why or when, and the action
Appears endless and ridiculous, we are all so ridiculous, we
Should all laugh ourselves silly at what desire would make

Of us all: one ridiculous body of bodies. And some think
This is what we are meant for, this *Garden of Earthly Delights*,
This is our truest delectation, freed from the penalties of denial,

And maybe Bosch's subject isn't literally Ghent's putative bathhouses
But the glee and anxiety I still feel even in my mid-fifties as life's flush
Fruit hangs, faces in boughs, remotely flashing come Sweetie, come taste me.

In the left-most panel everything starts. Adam, looking like a stiff
Or a Lazarus in need of raising, looks up at Eve, presented
To him by God (who is clothed). Everywhere the trees hang with
   pendulous

Superabundant apples, like the June Taylor Dancers dancing
Before the *Honeymooners— the moon-in-the sky, like a big
Pizza pie*—outside the barest of bare apartments, or like

Bunches of balls. Little creatures devour one another
In the foreground. (A cat's caught her mouse and drags its limp,
Tasty little corpse away. She prances.) Surely there is no

Such creature as the little one with a duck-bill and teeth.
Adam looks up at Eve and everything seems to start. But it's not
That easy, you see, when you close the cabinet of the triptych,

A proper parody, maybe, of an altarpiece, and see God, startled
And startlingly small before his creation, a *grisaille*, gray
Because there is not yet a sun or a moon and we have only

A charmed sphere of incipient being, which startles even God,
In this image, who wears a pope's triple-crown, and I want to laugh:
It's not a cynic's laughter, see, but a belly laugh from the belly's heart.

The Hawk

Old women cool their bodies' ovens
In the evening, in chairs, by the front door,
In the street, floral dresses stretched
Over their spread knees one of them slaps
Cackling in laughter, the sunset
Illumining the living room behind them
And—through the door—the three of them:
"Oh that guy, that cretin, what a *thief!*"
She stretches the word, stretches then drums it.
She echoes down high alleys into evening.

Pastoral Limerick

Like a battering ram
The suckling lamb
Shocks the dried udder
To flow and deliver:
(She lets it, a little.)
O answer the riddle
How weaning is learning
How loving is spurning.

Contra Artem

What's a song without measure,
Or a verse without meter,
Company without pleasure,
Savor, past, or future?
Say how your arts matter,
O Shell, o Inky Cipher,
Since spirit comes at leisure,
Its own place, time, and manner,
Why climb the ladder,
If scaffold and tower scatter
Shattering like chatter
And sitting ascends better?

Epigram

I caught I thought a hint of mint,
Or bee balm, purplish at the tips,
And leaning into it, I bent
Nettles brushing my nose and lips.

Jackdaws
(AWP: the pot calls the kettle black)

Those gregarious, garrulous big birds
All talking at once loudly at each other
In the great spruce, white blooms, and juniper
Hurl sounds with such inflection they're like words
My early morning reveries just make out
As a philological argument:
Careerists, red faced, Turks and Old Guard, shout,
Though, really, it's more the poets I meant:
Ten thousand strong, and more, to congregate
Each flying off to a room in which to read
At periodical intervals: insatiate,
All bright chit-chat, this need to preen and breed,
No "nest of fierties," we; see all we've wrought?
We're hurt, though, no one heeds us as they ought.

Pro Post Po Mo?

"the starry heavens above me and the moral law within me"
—Kant

I weary of the facile weariness.
That anti-idol's just another idol,
Another master narrative, no less

Historical than histories whose mess
Odious ideologies enable.
I weary of the facile. Weariness:

The easy, unctuous urges to confess
Always already what Cain did to Abel,
Another master (narrative no less

Defining) having led him to redress
One's unequal lot: envy's rocking cradle
I weary of. The facile weariness

Winks; night's stars (filter-feeding krill) fluoresce;
And ego's flares declare brutish rebuttal
Another master narrative. No less

Inhuman night, whose milky nakedness
Seems to me joy's heart's one staple,
I weary of the facile, weariness—
Another master: narrative, no less.

In the Dora Maar House
(Ménerbes, France)

Picasso the matelot, his Colt cocked,
Amiably inert in the photo
From Houston's museum studio,
Stares inured from his cell of glass.
And Dora, Red Dora, is signed in his hand:
Luminous Proteus, cut to the quick, here held.

This gorgeous attic of the world,
Cicadas in the pines, this red tiled-roof,
This massive joist, veined knobby pine
Ramming the ceiling end to end,
Cross-tied, lit windows stitched, stone-arched,
Make me an insect intellect
Bumbling and humming. Hear, my wings rasp.
My Queen, the dormant one, is gone
Deep in the rust of the charmed locks.

In Unity
(The Gift of the Magi)

The younger Brueghel's take on the scene
Confuses me at first; it's like the father's:
The cracked basement's here, the ruined choir
Of the old law blanketing with snow
But the milling crowds are gone
And this flashing of lances is new:

The shields and armor of Herod's army
Peer impercipient down an alley;
The three wise men laden with gifts; asses
(Blinkers and headpieces embroidered red)
Prance down the center
Of the little canvas to the child still
On the bottom-most corner edge of it all.

The mighty are blind. We are not
(Though we could be) threatened by these gifts,
This seems to say, we nevertheless see
Since he, the son, has recast himself
To shift, with his gift, the father's gift
So it's his as we slip and nothing's amiss.

Prague Suite, Modernist Baroque

"The whole period of Stalinist terror was a period of collective lyrical delirium."—Milan Kundera

"Je reste roi de mes douleurs"
—Louis Aragon

Where, oh song, would you soar
From this low door, from the green-domed
Strahof, its layered manuscripts,
Fourteenth-century Gospels in Czcch,
Exuberant ceilings—over the vineyard,
The many-spired, the many-domed
Center of the city with its bridges,
Chained Saint John rubbed bright
Bound in his shroud for his watery grave
Burnished by the fingers of tourists
On the buckle of the belt
Of the Bridge of Saint Charles,
"THE TEARS OF STALIN"
On the hill by the gold, winged bridge
(Piped-in electronic warbling
To split the eardrums of pigeons)
Over the flowing Vlatava?—

Who would I be who would sing
That soaring song, the ashes
Of Kalandra, martyred poet among
Many martyrs, Eluard the "great
Archangel" piped through
The City to sing the Justice
And Brotherhood for which his brother
Kalandra had to die, Kundera lamented,

Exiled, distrustful of all such *kitsch*
("The denial of shit"), soaring
Harmonious lyrics, the flames that licked
Jan Huss, who would not renounce
Simple truth or countenance
Crusades or Indulgences, city of Puppetry
And Irony, the German Catholic
Hapsburgs (now exiled) who built
This soaring beauty in triumph
Over heretical Czechs, the Temples
Emptied now, too, save the tourists: "I've
Had enough of this Jewish stuff,
I think, haven't you, Dear?" I hear.

Oh lyre, oh mistress of liars
Who would sing Truth,
Anathema sit, Instrument,
Sing New Town's low cobbled streets patterned
On the streets of Old Jerusalem
Watched by the Castle's lit-dark fortress-stone,
Consolation of hawkers proclaiming in teams
Mozart, Hayden (Berlioz even) sweet
To the ear, who'll finger you in their singing
Endlessly reiterated adagios,
Do we need you to cry out in pleasure
Predictably again that history
Might end? Aragon, True
To the end, and King of his miseries,
Style's miracles having made of him
A monument, yet another, a winding shell,
—Little bar—but oh, song, would that in you

Roma might share table with Turk
And Czech on the benches of the Strahof,

Vale of Tears, glitzy bitter-sweet forgetting,
Father and son barefooted in the shop window
Little fishes tickling their toes kissing them
Giggling for us to see that we might go in
And buy the goods, oh Song, can you point
Us out, pluck us, or teach us how to reach
Another country where each meets each,
Beyond the intimate little oubliettes of irony,
And *Kitsch*'s kitchens, among history's odious odors, or are we
Or must we be, or be mostly,
What Miró saw us as: genitals and teeth?

Palm Sunday in Marseille
(March 2005)

My folded palm frond in my pocket,
I take myself to lunch: couscous
Tunisian-style with lamb.
I sit, I loosen the noose

A bit, I listen to *malouf*
From Andalusia. This is good,
I think. The waiter—calm,
Green-eyed—has, like the neighborhood,

Grown on me, telling me how
His mother worked the cream
Into the grains with her hands
Dreaming of home: I eat it all up.

In All Saints, Marseille

My heart can't get up from itself.
The chapel I prayed in is cold.
My head only knows what it knows,

And God only shows what he shows.
(I'm told that the cold's in the stone.
We can't get the pilots to light.)

A motley imperial lot
We chat in the back after church
And nothing I hear turns out right.

A couple who fled from Vichy
Through Tunis to Portugal came
Home safely to England and then

The two of them lived through the Blitz:
The husband's been dead for five years.
Without him, his widow's a shade.

She conjures their love for my eyes:
Their granddaughter stands by her side
The image of youth she once was.

A journalist's friend tells me she's
Forgiven a murderer: hate
Can only repeat what it sees

(His murder revenge for the raids
On Tripoli Reagan unleashed).
She's free, "as he'd want her to be."

We finish our small-talk and tea.
The clicking space-heaters won't start.
Rumanian children at play

Have drawn whole new worlds in an hour.
Apocalypse knocks at the door.
We've kept him at bay. He can wait.

To the Last Century

Inhuman Nothingness, who could forgive
Non-being's being its last century
Of scribbling an incoherent missive
To the blinded that they need not worry
Or feel sorry, voiced over in no tongue
That's recognizable to anyone
Though old inflections' songs may still be wrung
In social hope, mad jests, all said and done.
Bitter aspersions cast down, all your crowns,
Ring, bells, split listening, with the glass blown out,
May the boys' bones lie clean, done their break downs,
Forget what you're about opening the spout
Everything melting the flesh of the leaf
Like snow-white belief down cold-veined grief.

Singularity

And so now we should all await the singularity,
Our neurons will be augmented by nanobots so
All the lovely firing of our brains will be restrained
To frame the architecture of thought, mind itself
Altered too, retaining more of itself and uploaded

Elsewhere in conversation with other thoughts,
Though otherness itself will become an empty
Category in the melding, bodies made as shapes
Thought might animate, though whose thoughts
These would be is to me a mystery, but what

Do I know about all this, or the gradual expansion
Of consciousness through the material world,
Beyond our solar system, as consciousness
Collected expands to embrace, to give itself
Like grace that first called the universe into being

Though maybe, I grant you, we swing through
Multi-verses, strings humming billions of infinitesimal
Songs to bring into being the particular nature
Of each atom each inhabits, and grace must bring
To itself another in relation and be known, though

How this will be I cannot see, not everything
I see or feel locked into perpetuity, thank goodness,
Nor shared, and we have reached the end of history,
I read, the thought-meme of liberty surviving
To reproduce itself, gone viral, and now democracy

Infects all of humanity, and a care for the weak,
Perhaps we are evolving soon beyond war, murder
And want, and there is nothing we can do to stop this,
History is so good in its unfolding, but I am skeptical,
Odd little avatars governing the postings popping

Up continually on screens, my students feeling
Anguish, they have so many friends and know
So much about all of them, we are so alone and sad,
They say, in their streaming play all night and day,
So maybe I should hear strings spinning invisible

Sympathy though I'll confess fear of being one of the last
New Neanderthals, ice melting, the new taking our place,
Viciously efficient, to hear traces of us, maybe, but
I'll wager we'll all chatter and grow closer in our going,
Song realigning time taking everything God knows where

And in the meanwhile I'll style stars spinning in the air
That touches them tonight not in the least as sparkling
Color, the metaphorical strings dark matter hurtles
With us, ramping-up, slowly, home, as I'm pulled tight
As a bowstring, I know, bent by what I'm meant to hit.

TRANSLATIONS

From *Bestiary*

(1911) Guillaume Apollinaire

Horse

My hard formal dreams will bestride you,
My fate your gold car's handsome coachman
Who, for reins, will hold, drawn to frenzy,
My lines, paragons of all poetry.

Hare

Don't be lascivious and timid
Like the hare and the enamored.
But may your brain be always
The pregnant doe who conceives.

Mouse

These beautiful mornings, mouse of time,
You slowly nibble through my life. I'm
Going to be (God!) twenty-eight,
Having lived badly, not as I'd hoped.

Elephant

As an elephant has his ivory
I have in my mouth a treasured good.
Purple death! . . . I buy my glory
At the cost of melodious words.

Louse

Lice, friends, lovers even,
All who love us, they're cruel!
For them all our blood runs.
The beloved are miserable.

Grasshopper

Behold the slender grasshopper,
Saint John's supper.
May my lines be like that
On which the best feast.

Orpheus

May your heart be the bait and the sky the pool!
Because, fisherman, what fresh or even salt-water fish
Is there that equals, both in shape and flavor,
This beautiful heavenly fish, which is JESUS, My savior?

Dolphin

Dolphins, you play in the ocean.
But always bitter, the flow you move through.
Does my joy break out on occasion?
Life is cruel too.

Octopus

Throwing his ink at the heavens,
Sucking the blood of his loves

And finding the whole thing delicious,
I am this inhuman monster.

Jellyfish

Jellyfish, unlucky heads
With purple hair
It's in storms that you find pleasure
And like you I take pleasure there.

Crawfish

Uncertainty, oh my pleasures,
You and I we all disappear together
As the crawfish scatter
Backwards, backwards.

Carp

In your tanks, in your ponds,
Carp, may you live long!
Does death forget you, fish
Of wretchedness?

Orpheus

The female halcyon,
Love, and flying Sirens,
Know deadly, dangerous
And inhuman songs.
Heed not these cursed birds,
But the Angels of paradise.

Sirens

Did I know where, Sirens, your boredom originates
When you moan, far way, in the night?
Sea, I am like you, full of set voices
And my singing ships are called years.

Owl

My poor heart is an owl
Nailed, un-nailed, nailed again.
Its blood, its ardor exhausted.
Praised be all those who love me.

Ibis

Yes, into the earthly shadow I'll
Go, oh certain death, so be it!
Deadly Latin, horrid word:
Ibis, bird from the banks of the Nile.

Bull

This cherubim speaks plaudits
Of paradise, where, amongst angels,
We shall live again, my dear friends all,
When the good Lord permits it.

From *The Passion Rendered in Parts*
(ca. 1623) George Herbert

I. To the dying Lord

Since so many wounds defeat tears and two eyes,
    And I'll be no match, even quite turned into tears;
Let ink flow, a fitter liquid for sins
    And now with its own hue let my fault weep.

II. On the bloody sweat

To what place, o sweat, shall you flee? although another part of Christ
    May know no limit; a small vein, that is your room.
If that wondrous body to you should not prove pleasing,
    All the more, perforce, would the crowd displease you:
Unless perchance you seek me out: for by just as much as
I am more unworthy myself, you
    by coming to help me worthier can be.

IX. On the Whip

O Christ, the scourged world's hope and victory,
    When charges swell, and my penalty approaches,
Sweetly bring to me the whip known to you in the flesh.
    Let the shadow of your rod more often suffice.
Act mercifully: Delicate consciences double the strokes against themselves
    And their lashes are their own mild hearts.

X.   On the divided garments

If, O Christ, while you're fixed with nails to the cross, your clothes
        Are your enemies' bequest, not your friends',
As custom demands; what will you give to your own? Yourself.

XV.   On his Bowed head. (John xix.30)

Wild foxes have caves, and nests are at hand for birds,
        And each knows its own bed, its own lair.
Yet Christ, the sort to give shelter, lacks a host; he only has,
        Hung from the cross, a spot against which to bow his head.

XVIII. Earthquake

If you are fixed, yet the Earth stirs: since, with the Cross, you can
        Carry all encompassed; even so once Sampson bore the doors.
Alas, inert people, first fasten the fleeting Earth,
        Only then assault the Lord with spikes.

From *Sacred Grove*

(ca. 1623) George Herbert

V.   On Holy Scriptures

Alas, what spirit, and ardent whirlwind
Governs my entrails, and turns over
In my inmost breast my thoughts?
Have I by sitting by the doors
At evening inhaled a shooting star,
What's more does she, not knowing how
To lie entirely hidden in a foul lodging
Consider an escape?
Did I in eating honey, eat the bee
Swallowing with her home as well the queen?
But no, no bee or star stings me,
Most Holy Paper, it was you
Who travelled through my heart's hidden
Recesses and blind hallows, and all its alleys
And the bends of my fleeting desire.
Ah, how sly you are at crossing
Its mountain passes, its meandering
And coils, how skilled you are.
The power that built, knows its own house.

VIII. On Washing the feet of the Apostles

The Ancients contend the Sun rose from the Ocean
        After refreshing himself each night in icy waters:
More truly was this done, Christ, once when you washed
        What ringed the whole world round, those feet.

IX. On Saint Luke

Why did God choose a Doctor, who spirit-filled
    Might write Christ's deeds with a holy hand?
So each might learn for himself what was fit: plainly harmful,
    O sad Adam, the green tree-fruit proved to you.

XII. The Storm with Christ sleeping

As you sleep, the sea rises: as, O Christ, you rise again
    The sea sleeps: how well the reins you hold!

XIX. Affliction

The waves on which you walked, Christ, batter me,
    And vault above my head, which lay beneath your feet.
Christ, if over the waves I cannot wander:
    Through waves at least, vouchsafe that I myself may wade.

XX. On Vain-Glory

Whoever with a restless spirit sucks up idle talk
And seeks out gassy glories,
Steps outside the peak of joy,
And throws it away, too, through as many heads
As the boorish crowd carries.
Instead really get it together, and stand up for yourself;
Draw tighter life's bags with a short knot,
Perfectly compact in yourself, for if you're arms akimbo,
A thousand fights, a thousand cheats will grasp
And lead you till, falling on your helmet
A thousand noses, a thousand bellies laugh at you.
So as a savvy sailor draw in your sails

And neither blow off nor suck up fame:
Holding your actions in balance:
What glory a crowd might bring, restrain;
If a crowd should cut off glory, let it.
A morose person makes sour, clotted milk:
A light one, watery rennet curds.

XXIII. A Consolation

Why do you cry and sigh late, laggard sighs, as if
      Your friend's dark death just happened now?
From the cradle Death's sentence daily slits
      All of our throats, nor does any die just once.
We live but now: no one can live life
      Yesterday: yesterday's life is buried today.
Nestor did not pass through, but died, three hundred years,
      Or more exactly he lives so many in dying so many.
As you weep, life flees: your weeping is for you a water-clock,
      And each tear-drop measures its matching deaths.
So in vain you're astonished at one more among so many deaths,
      This tear will come too late, if cry you will.
Cease your weeping and moans: since by these showers
      And breezes, you can't bring back the flesh's flower.
Nor should you grieve for your friend, who's fled to that
      Height, where no one for you can mourn.

XXIV. On Angels

The Angels' full-grown awareness
Has no resemblance to our own, which requires
For an essence to be given, that we ask a sense:
And unless eyesight unseal the door
And our millstones bestow the meal,

Often it nothing useful threshes out of itself.
And far indeed from us distanced
Flow the rivers of understanding:
If not through essence, we cannot by ourselves,
What we in essence are, attain by thought.
Not so great is the Angel's travel to the waves,
By no circuitous route do they pierce what's to be known,
For them perpetual windows lie open,
Themselves through themselves thus easily knowing
And they themselves are for themselves millstones and meal.

XXIX. A Reasonable Sacrifice

If you pondered the origin of both Altars and Humans,
      Living Earth was a Man: dead Earth, an Altar:
Those which apart do harm, through Christ's seal, in one
      Thing co-align; & Man is made God's living Altar.

XXX. Thomas the Twin

While with his fingers your servant actually pushes
Into you, even to such revelation do you submit?
You are of course complete love, love's marrow,
You who, for slow faith and a shallow mind
Prepare a welcome, and a fragrant bed,
Where one may hide, and turning about, envelop oneself
As in a dependable inn and strong citadel,
Lest the roaring Lion dispatch him as he rambles.

XXXI. On a Sundial

The bridal of the Sky and Earth this emblem shows
      To the Sky is due light, and shade to the ground:

So Human mass rests both on soul and body,
    Whose origin from opposite places flowed.
Reflect, wicked one, on how much terror ground
    Without light, or flesh without mind would hold.

XXXII. Death's Triumph
[written after the beginning of the Thirty Years' War]

O my hand, a force to marvel at, and my deathless belly! Which neither
The roiling river Emathius, nor Daunia running rich with blood,
Not the twice three thousand progeny of slaughter, could satisfy,
The world's courses less than our gut and engorging.
The ancients are said to live in oaks, and then caves
Growing in number together with their offspring:
Nor am I shut out, however: for from one tree life
An acorn gave, and the trunk a dwelling, and the shoots death.
        Meanwhile, the young began to gather from far and wide
                        for Flora's Festival
With the farmers freed from worry and plows:
The crossroads begin to boil up with feet, the air with shouts.
As they lay here on the grass, one of the more caustic
Turns up his nose at everything, and provokes his companions:
                        an Ucalegon
Won't take it, and ferociously with trenchant words he volleys back:
The reproaches to his slit side cling.
The crowd is split like crossroads into parts.
Anger makes a weapon, and the world is furor's very storehouse.
Bacchus feeds brawls; to drinkers everything
But life is double; one of them knocked down by rocks, another
With burnt stakes, one faction pours its life into cups,
Another into platters; wine's fickleness rages
With blood, what it had given stripping away. Such were
Death's beginnings: thus as a young girl played Tisiphone.

Crude and unskilled slaughter did not delight; deftness
In Death is demanded, and a disciplined murderer esteemed.
Hence a soldier's first campaign, a young man accustomed to little,
And Bellona is molded, and mock-ups made of true battle,
And battle lines drawn up and winters spent in animal skins,
And all this so they may slash ribs open and not be judged,
And be called masters of the art of murder, and death's disciples.
Surely indeed a new recruit who rehearses well at the stake
Kills a thousand enemies, if his intent alone must be considered.
Alas, pitiful men! Who pursues as much true virtues
As slaughter? So must you kill six hundred
To feed one life? However the hydra of inflicting injury grows,
Sadly, and where iron from the inmost earth is severed,
The crime's fecund steel, already dyed with blood,
Cannot be filled, and it consumes the World.
Why should I tell again war's weapons, with which a prior world bristled:
And Balistas and Onagers or what the savage Scorpion
Or Catapults can do, and the inventions of the Sicilian Master,
And the English bows, rejoicing in a Frenchman's blood,
And the Fusibali sling-shots, relying on which, with Divine Force,
Godlike Tityrus laid low the Idumaean enemy?
Add also chariots and, with a British wagon-pole,
Arviragus, and axle-scythes that mow down what stands in the way,
Why even the Battering Ram brings ruin, and Demetrius with great art:
So in the past they killed.
         Still the world lacked what was most worthy for men's vices
The engine, which no age will ever curse enough;
Glowing metal in the glazing furnace melts,
And fluid iron flows through the accustomed pipes:
Out comes the tube, and in the likeness of Homer's Cyclops
A one-eyed prodigy it is, and pleased with its central opening.
From thence the support of wheels and an axle, as if a curule chair
On which sits Death himself over humanity triumphant,
Fiery dust rises, cast forth from the paneled ceilings

Of Orcus, of the infernal board the precious sweetmeats,
From the sulfurous lake, and with all Mephitis imbued.
To this added a ball shaped like an Acorn, the one that antiquity
Is believed to disgorge, before with a favoring divine power fruits were planted.
An acorn ball of lead, and livid as if of its own fault conscious,
Pluto's blood-red minister, the letter of Fate
In lead sealed, and sundering life's distaffs and threads,
Since aged Atropos's arms are drooping.
            When these things were accoutered, the servant draws near
                                   with a live cord,
And raising his deadly right hand, with which the lit flax is touched lightly
With the wind, he lights a piece with the tinder
Of hellish dust: the fire once taken leaps and tosses
All matter: Tisiphone no longer constrains herself to her cave;
Crowned with flame and false lightning
She rushes forth, and reveling like a bacchant raises a hideous clamor.
The shrill rattle grows deafening, and cracks all the heavens and Tartarus.
No longer is any Music celestial to be heard
Or the groans of Erebus: turning itself in a pitch-black whirlwind
And belching forth all cloud, the Acorn rushes forth from the depth
Headlong: cities fall, with horror walls
Explode, and the fragile high attic of the world creaks.
Recumbent over the whole plain a thousand lifeless bodies lie
From but one blow: not thus does a plague, not thus a star with a fatal
Flash annihilate: see, the Stygian Skiff groans
With throngs, and the weary Toll-taker prays for aid.
Nor does the Acorn alone harm; at some time the flying
Blast whispers death, and the air the life that it nourished withdraws.
            Recount, you Furies, in what origin the Monster exults.
Night, Aetna, and Chaos, Night begot as the first ones.
Aetna gave birth to Cacus vomiting fire, who then Ixion
By many sung begot, then Ixion commingling with black clouds
Begot a Monk, who inhabiting the cheerless threshold
Of a dark cell, full of night and the Devil,

First with powder brought forth this frightful monster.
Who would deny that Monks meditate on death, and concern
                                                    themselves
With doleful dust, and are lowly, and that such dejected things,
Even those things that belong under the very earth, to their
                                                    hearts are dear?
        Nor did our attack however halt here for a bit: a Jesuit arose
Worse than all war's engines, and hurls at the World lightning,
Laughing at the contemptible Canons, which destroy bodies
Not souls, and are embellished with the rarified blood of kings,
Clamorous with a foolish noise, and confessing their crime,
        Here I fix my power's apex: for mortals in body and soul
It is finished. Let the Entire Earth serve me.

XXXIII. The Triumph of the Christian: against Death

Ah, really? You declaim such great things? By Hercules and Pollox,
Such a magnificent hawker you are, a renowned murderer.
What will I do for myself? I'm not the sort to hold tree-sized stakes
Against you, nor bows, or scorpions, or chariots,
Or swords, or Catapults may I wield, no, nor even
Mock slaps nor Battering Rams? What then? The Lamb and the
                                                    Cross.

XXXIV. On leaning-upon-the-breast John

O come on, gorger, move, so I may suck too:
So will you take for yourself the whole breast?
Do you block the spring that open lies for all?
Instead since rather for me he poured blood too,
And thence by law my right to the breast claimed
I demand the milk rolling down with blood;

So that, if such great favor should be mixed
With my sin's remission, falling in death
On his shoulder even the very Throne Seats I would assail.

XXXV. To the Lord

O Christ, the glory, sweetness, and near a hundred Hyblas,
The heart's apex, my soul's battle and peace,
Let me truly see you; as often as I'll say, now, let me see;
Let me die, o my life, in your eyes.
If permitted, and I'll die: or if your vision is life,
Why go on, near death in prayer, without you?
Ah, let me see; do you think I see you,
Who used to heal the blind, though I do not see?
I mean to swear I don't see; or, if this is blocked,
What's about to happen prevent with your look.

THE END
Glory be to God Alone

from **WATCH** (2009)

From the Heights

My vision is partial, my voice middling, and I do not trust myself to the heights
though everything here below begins to mingle and seem to me part of one
    canvas:
ego, self-delusion, and pride in an infinite hall of mirrors with reflection

mirroring all the old self-deceptions masquerading as penitential retractions.
As I ride the bus up the mountain, the water below is no longer white as at dawn
when I looked out and felt as if glimpsing the hem of heaven's wedding dress.

Earlier even, walking before dawn, I heard one bird singing to itself and wondered
to myself whether it was a caged bird on someone's balcony in the early cold
till warbling began to answer in another tree across the street and then

suddenly a mounting crescendo of other songs loudly greeting the morning not yet
arrived, welcoming it into light, into the full presence of day, after which I hear
nothing but traffic and the noises that people make going about their daily
    business.

The driver tells me of his town near Spain, north of Toulouse, where *Louis Treize*
tried to kill all the Protestants, where the former president of the Spanish Republic
was buried during the civil war because he could find no peace at home. (Aragon

and Picasso fled to France, as well, Aragon leaving his mother speech to sing
the nightingale's slaughter.) The town still bears the scars of the King's
    bombardments.
We climb higher and higher. I think of Daourt's paintings, of the blue openings

that appear so often in them. The labyrinth of scaffolding in one, workmen
transfixed in the middle of their labor, and in lonely apartments across the way
a woman hidden in impossible contortions, and everywhere sad, magisterial cats

looking at us questioningly. Even in her studio, the crossing lines of light and
        shadow,
despite her large, open work space, feels like a spider web of work, the rectangular
blue above and the light caught in a high window—glimpses of transcendence.

During the Occupation, Daourt was protected in the house of the Comtesse in
        Marseille,
but after liberation, her mind grew worse until she began to dress in newspapers
and beg in the streets. I climb another hill in Nice to the Chagall Museum

where a young Japanese artist asks me (I don't know why) the significance
of the "arc-en-ciel" and whether there's a biblical story. I say that God destroyed
the world in a flood yet promises never to flood the world again. *It means hope.*

In the next room, I stand before *L'Exode.* Christ hangs in the cross high in the
        center
but a flood of people moves up and to the left through fire, a blue woman suckling
her child, hopelessly, buildings falling in fire, an artist, head turned unnaturally

backwards from the window, framed by the cross in the glass (no, this is another
painting I'm remembering), a spectral virgin floating towards death, a mother
        and child
born into a sea of floating, drowning faces, and the Christ glowing in a white
        nimbus,

his face dark in contrast. I look back and forth from the slaughter (a child put down
on the ground by his mother beside a little billy goat looking up to the hand
        stroking it.)
Christ's right eye is gouged, I think. Then, no: *If thy right eye offend thee,*
                        pluck it out.

Digs
(Marnay-sur-Seine, Champagne)

The menhir in a blue field of wheat
cuts a yellow line of rapeseed and the white
lips of recycling pits.

I walk to the darkened holes
of log poles, a long house, Neolithic, the pit
of pottery shards and bone pits, to the dark
hardened place that held fire.
                    Yesterday
I startled a red fox near the road. It leapt fire
                    from tuft
        to tuft
into a thicket.
        I suckle on signs,
a sparrow hawk heckling a heron,
the heron spinning slowly before lifting.

Merovingian graves: a mother and two children
knees to chest in earth *ova*—and I think
much more of me may remain than I had thought or hoped.

On the sarcophagus, white waves, chiseled grain
in wind at an angle, a brass buckle,
an iridescent vial;
                tumuli, circles in a circle;
an iron age granary;
                a Roman road.
I imagine angles, eyes, who made what's made,
hands holding stone, bronze, or iron,
or flesh and bone alone, clutches of people,

transfiguring spirits and tongues,
what I speak, eat, and feel made up of bits of them
so grain's good, birth first, and the fresh fruit sweet:
it isn't their ends any more than them I meet.

River

A loon dives in the swollen river.
It followed the river first.
The town lies between it and canals
Diverted from the river.
The beak of the loon is orange,
Its wingspan broader than a duck's.

My father's legs were swollen.
His once thin ankles barely fit his shoes.
His heart no longer fed his body.
Toxins and liquids began to drown him.
His silly doctors didn't see
He couldn't breathe.

My father took me to the river.
We fished for bass and bluegill,
Sunfish, cats. Fat suckers,
Their lips like suction cups,
We put back. Too many little bones
to catch and make you choke.

I no longer want to go fishing.
I don't even want to play
In the water. The boat
Here has no oars, the current
Is too swift. In the dark, teenagers
Discover their body together.

The body feels like a prison.
I kneel by my father's stapled body.
He suctions thick liquid from his lungs.

He coughs to clear them; it hurts.
He wants more air. He wants
To live, the heart's valve's parachutes

Opening with oxygen to feed
The body's healing. A tube
Empties the chest cavity. He excretes
Liquids and poisons.
His shocked kidneys come to life.
His stunned heart beats. His lung

Opens again. He eats. He poops.
He walks. He wants to go home.
On the phone, I catch my sister
Taking him home. It's snowing.
It's cold. My brother and mother
Help him climb the stairs.

I walk down the path
By the shallow canal. I see
A falcon fishing. The power plant
Breathes steam. I hope
The wind won't singe me.
I come to the falls

Where a little dog
Barks and bounces hello. His owner
Smiles and greets me. In the church
Of Saint Laurence I kneel, I
Give thanks, my heart jumps.

Excess
(after Henri Michaux)

I've pushed the door open inside.
I'm here, already, to give you
What you've been needing, what you want

So badly it makes you ache. Take
That sudden illness dropped like lead—
I lift it. I act. My joy's this

Quick. Cuts, stitched, heal, and fever falls.
Hair grows back. Food tastes good.
I stop that superabundance

Of cells. Now only good excess
Greets you with smiles and ease.
You sit in the sun. The carafe

Of water reflects the windows
You can't see, peripheries
Possibilities opening!

You drink them in the sun, happy.
You enjoy the company
Of those you don't know and those

You love, too, here with you.
There is time. Old voices that say
You'll have nothing to offer

I shut them all up.
I show them the door where they will
Be able to cripple only

Themselves with malice. I free you
Too from that malice. You pity them.
You are able to be

Happy in this cool sun.
Slanderers do not
Envy you. (You've done nothing

To merit their anger.) Your conscience is
Light and when able
You've made amends, nor have you

Hidden knives in apologies.
I give you work with a purpose
You've chosen. Anxiety

Doesn't keep you up. When the Black
Ox treads on you his heavy hooves
Don't teach you the wrong things.

(Without him, are we less?)
You welcome love. You grab the lock
Of the child as he comes and don't

Love Chance's ugly butt.
You are not impatient in grief.
Such grief as you meet's a measure

Of love. I wash your future face.
The logjam's broken.
Pleasure flows in again

Through these banks more
Than you thought possible.
I give you this robin's egg blue

Left in the grass to take. I'll say
hello in the morning. We can meet
friends and walk if you like.

Watch

We pass the straits of the Cape
where grazing whales gather,
though they're not, I'm told, social
creatures by nature.

Alice asks how they can sleep
if they must think to breathe.
Cranial hemispheres wink and wake
and alternate,

so whales are half-awake
and half-asleep, balanced between each
of our states
through dive and breach.

Once on the kitchen wall
of a dune shack I saw,
like a headdress,
the baleen of a whale—

frayed filaments
run from a thin,
curled, rib-like bone:
sieves for the sea.

Like this sickle-moon fin
"negatively buoyant"
I sink in sleep,
but end, I think, where I begin.

Following one as it leaves
two other whales we see
suddenly not what we're heading for
but the asymmetrically

colored snout of a fin whale
as it rises parallel
within a stone's
throw of the boat,

the great eye set back
water crashing rushing
to let me see where it ought to be.
I lose track,

the mottled chin's marble
veined, swirling
through its green veil, which
the top jaw slits.

And then, that's it,
I think. Nights I'm thrown
upright from my rest. Brine
thumps my chest.

Sens

Christ's the dark pistil (five red petals point)
Transecting with golden bars the bass viol,
His consort's honeycomb, in counterpoint
As red moves toward me through my blue denial
Above the abandoned Samaritan,
The fall, the law, as if his sacrifice
Transfuses hives with the honey that ran
Straight from the center like a fragrant spice.
The facing apse: lids pop and people pccp,
Full bodied, from graves. They are whole again
Though this window's not: blank-pocked. Devils leap
Down: red, blue (finned?). The loved, in lines, walk in,
Or walk together on the way they know
Will show the way, or this is what they show.

Wake

(Mississippi, September 2005)

I

In the wake of the eye, our oak cracks one thick
Limb on a pivot, then lifts, about to split.
From the dark we watch the neighbor's pear splay,
Wind fling green pecans, wires block the driveway,
One low black wire (alive?) swinging the road.

Water breaches the levies on our
Five-inch black-and-white. A woman floats
A plastic crate. The weak die at the airport,
At Charity, on rooftops, attended,
In attics, when our screen goes out, a bullet.

II In the Coliseum

*"One of my sons is afflicted. Where is
My Nana?"* he asks me. *"What can I say
To him?"* he asks me. A stuttering woman
Sits by her sister. *"Oh, is she drowning!"*
I don't know what I'm doing and I won't.

III

Troops man roadblocks. Hurricane odor (sweet sour):
Mold in the playroom, mold in the tiles,
On dolls, toys, clothes, and books. My head, a child's
Swing, turns a hinge-song, rain crow, rotted crown.

Caravaggio's *Saint Ursula*

My flight is due to board in a few hours.
It will take me an hour, I calculate, once
I have left the exhibit, to buy my ticket,
catch the train, and reach the terminal so I
cut to the last room first because of the crowds
noticing in passing the Archangel's fierce eye
as he stands over Mary praying, head bent.

In another painting, Saint Ursula seems already
dead, though still conscious, almost green.
Her executioner has just let fly his arrow
at close range, and his well-dressed buddies
behind her, one in armor, don't even seem focused on what
has just happened. The old man's eyes seem wise
and yet untroubled. It's all very disorienting,
and I want to look behind me where they're looking
but despite myself follow Ursula's eye. The painter
has given the blur of the shaft as if both passing
and already passed and the first red gush
that I have had to stand still, and close, to see
in the crowd with the painter, no saint,
gasping as if struck through as he strikes.

Capital Towers

"I do not tell you these stories
so that you will feel sorrow
for my private losses,

but so you will understand
more and so be able
to make others understand."

Deng pauses. He and Agot address
the Coffee Club, on the top floor
of Capital Towers, overlooking

the Governor's mansion, Statehouse,
the decaying, grand
King Edward, and the Electric Building—

the last gutted like a fish,
its art deco scales intact and buffed
lustrous against brown marble.

My eye, intent ever
on artifice, wanders. I am a crow
with an eye for shiny things,

or am I like the decadent Roman
patron from Fellini's Petronius
who'd pay a poor man to let him

watch us have his
hand cut off? *You recoil?*
Well, so do I. But no,

no, this surely isn't why the gentleman
takes Agot's hand in both his and says,
"You've got quite a story. Thank you

for telling it to us." We mean
well, we all do mean well,
imagining ourselves or our families

wandering unprotected and wanting
more than anything
to be the protector, to stave

off harm. Brecht
hated tragedy because it gave
pleasure to an audience that instead

of *pathos* needed a new way
of seeing, not moving
endings or gutless facades. Change.

Salvation

Young Dinka seminarians ask
Will God save the Muslims?
And those who sacrifice to gods—
The god of the spear, the god of the drum—
Or to the hungry ancestors?

Their teacher has been feeding them Tillich,
Barthes, and Daly, Thomas and Luther.
She cannot say,

"Finger not my treasure." (Herbert quipped
Through God's voice breaking the locks
Of the double covenant.)

When Ignorance forded the river quickly
To God, tinker Bunyan dispatched him
To Hell by infernal elevator.

When the people took Christ as their savior
The drum before which some
Left watches and little gifts
Of thanksgiving was burned to ashes.
"It was part of our heritage! It's lost forever!"
Lost, too, the fleet spear that traveled
From village to village.

Father Mark, "Father Elephant" in Dinka,
Wrote of his friendships with believers
Of the traditional religions.
Deprived of their talk, he felt diminished.
He did not deny their criticisms.

Deng's grandfather holds still to the old religion.
Once, he came home drunk.
Deng gave his grandfather a shower
And put him to bed. "My bad grandson
Baptized me! He made me a Christian!"
He would not be convinced or consoled.
His grandfather would not be taken
To a Christian heaven. That place
Would strip him of all the loving flesh
With which his spirit held communion.

Strasbourg

The yellow and green rose, and the pink rock,
The chestnuts blooming, the cobblestone square,
Our Lady's tower rising everywhere,
Dark timbered fronts; the mechanical clock
Whose rooster crows three times for Peter's flock,
The Apostles, the old man's and the child's share
Of time—aspire I'd say to make me stare
And stop. I praise what I might otherwise mock,
The locked contingencies, the stock of losses,
Bright liquidity everywhere channeled,
A storied cityscape of destinies
Averted as when, turning, a young Turk tosses
His hands in the air and my chest's pummeled,
"My brother, forgive me!" and my thoughts freeze.

Protection

The Security
Chief
seems always

angry. He wants
to protect me.
I'm not fair.

We're both angry.
He's right.
I won't stand

on my
merit. Degrees
are "academic."

He e-mails us all
on 9/11 Lincoln's
prayer

(1863)
when the blood
of sons

and fathers
was shed
for "national sins":

"*Before the offended
Power,
to confess. . . .*"

On the Sunday
after, Philip's our
crucifer. Towering

over us, he beams
to lead the processional. One
refugee says, "They

followed us here. We
brought this danger
to you," as if any guilt

felt whatever its
merit might answer
powerlessness.

Common Ways
(Little Gidding, Cambridgeshire)

Near Saint John's Church, a ridge,
A Roman road, where people drove
Cattle to Cambridge market,
Pheasant roam the rows and roads.
Everywhere ancient common ways:
From Sawtry, through the fields, a path
(Across a field of yellow)
Still on a local map, with gates
That you might take and close.

Different bricks give evidence
Of age and order. Near the altar
Everything's oldest, and they brought
The altar itself down to stand
Among the people with the priest
Who faced them, to their north.

These were no Roman epicures.
Like them, though, set apart,
They left the state to its designs
And in a web of friendship held
Trembling, the fly of greed,
Mortifying the body's need,
Measuring their meat with weights,
"Watches," praying the psalms at night,
Nicholas sleeping on a board—
Medicine, bandages for the poor.
Poor boys who learned their Psalters earned
Pennies to spend or hoard.

Women with scissors bound and glued
Counter-Reformation prints
With Gospel passages to make
A book of "Harmonies."
Playing Socratic dialogues
They wrote in character
(In history they read
The hand of God in enemies
Rewarded for humility)
And musical interludes
In the Great Room, long since burned down,
Some "40 paces from the Church."

The King and court they fled
Came to them near the end.
Before Hampton Court or the trial
Charles sought solace here.

They passed their manuscripts with friends,
Susanna's found in George's hands
After he died. Nicholas, too,
Died early, his disease
Chronicled in letters as
Inscrutable as symptoms marked
By spots and agues, his despair
Doubled by the will's remorse.

Bathsheba thought them all rank mad
And fled after her husband's death
To London, on a wagon, in the hay,
John's brother Nicholas
In the end burning
The plays and poems of his youth.
The fires set the locals talking

Of witches, spells, and devils.
Prayer, valid everywhere,
By grace is the place
In which they rest and race.

In green April, I make my pilgrimage,
Smoke from refuse rising before
Prospects of hills and two spires,
The small pond winking through a copse,
Knee-high grass over the leaning stones,
Broken, illegible lines
Bowing to kiss their dust; inside—
An eagle (on which sits
The still Word) cleansed of the mire
Of the small pond, full centuries
Of water, lustrous brass again.
Talons on rock, the eagle lifts,
Resolute, stoic, in a sty
Where Mother Ferrar made their table,
The idol of iconoclasts
And heaven's honey, the heart's rest,
Exiled hope and wilderness.

Pilgrim

Near Trastevere, I found (finally)
San Agostino, maps approximate
At best, names changing block by block, the feet,

The dirty soles, of Caravaggio's pilgrims
Who bowed to Mary, and the marble floor's
Polychrome under my feet shone near

The body of the martyr Benedict
And Monica, the mother of *Confessions*.
In Santa Maria in Trastevere,

Mary is dead, and in the background
Christ held his mother childlike in his arms
But in a side niche, to the altar's left

Peter hung headlong not to mock his Lord's cross
With a crude look of confusion on his face
Or terror, the painter's execution crude

Power not Northern Gothic, startlingly
Small: its own kind. A chapel's cupola,
Elegant, Age of Reason, drew my eye

Up until standing beside Saint Joseph
Covered with butterflies, small folded notes
And Polaroids of people needing healing,

I felt as if I stood in Old New Spain,
The *Papagos'* (now *Tohono O'Odham*),
Lit candles in the Mission of San Luis,

A sixteenth-century wooden saint stretched out,
Recumbent agony with grief appended,
The pictured tubes and wires of old age

Or youth, two angels over the crossing
Dressed in white dresses, prayers at mass mixed with
The Moon and Sun and Wind, wild worldly forces

Whose spirits move and dance across the sky
As when, last night, my fireplace whined with force
Banging my shutters to get in. Before

I found the church of Saint Cecelia, who,
Beheaded patroness of music, lies
Silently white, face down, I walked through parts

Of Rome a little rougher, though still safe.
I felt safe, braced by a small town's distrust
Of the unknown. A wedding would take place

That afternoon. People were sweeping,
Unfolding carpets, setting up bouquets
Of flowers brightly arranged for the day

When I walked down into the crypt, my fee
In the palm of a sweet young African nun
in habit. Then, *oubliettes* like the hole

Villon was thrown down, but now I forget
Whether the Temple of Minerva led
Past the paste gems, the Roman home

Valerian knew, frescoes in the church
"like water after too much sweet," to quote
One patron. Now I'm getting all mixed up.

What did I see where? San Clemente's layers
—Familiar, incomplete—compete: Mithras,
The sun god, in a corner. Near the house

Still used when Emperor Constantine
Constructed a Creed and his new capitol,
I saw where you'd share meals in friendship

And bring a god to earth. An Irish guide
Planted his group. Looking to him, they blocked
The view inside. The house spring's gurgling still.

I ate a passable meal of lamb
Pasta with chicken at *Op!la!* that night
By myself. The waiter and I spoke French.

I made it an early night, watching the BBC's
World News report on indigenous cultures
And globalization. New roads cut old nets.

Home

"*Agot*: the name means *Cobra*" (at the dinner table
after Dinka services, we're joking about names
and their meanings), though

actually it means more *this* (Agot, who will
study radiology, crooks his hand and wrist to imitate
the shape a cobra might make when standing

to strike). They have to pause and
translate this for me and Mary Ann, who's done
the cooking, since we've been wondering why they're

laughing so hard. (She raised a family of boys
she tells me, elbows on the table, smiling.)
I'll get it wrong, though. When they tell

stories, I usually remember
only the end and beginning: the man
who throws a spear at a monkey for the pure

fun of scaring the monkey, in the end
caught between a crocodile
and the vengeful monkey who has his own turn

at *fun*—or the father who, gorging himself
for the *fattest man competition* and who also simply
loves to eat, comes to a village festival

to be disappointed that it is mostly dancing
and courting and that the food after must be shared,
who eats an entire whale that has been stranded

on the river, having sent his gluttonous son
away on a wild goose chase so that he might
eat everything himself, which he does, *end*

of story. Laughter. Why do they tell these stories
after dancing for the first time in the nave of the church,
moving in a circle and leaping many feet

into the air? I have never seen them smile
so or glow, whirled by a distant center. (Reverend
Woja tells me that for a few minutes

they are all home again in Africa.) The Somali
Muslim woman they've brought with them seems
happy, too. (Abuk, who is with her, speaks Arabic.)

But I started all this talking about Agot
and cobras and food and got carried away.
Before the thirsty had plenty, Moses,

with the snake that had eaten Pharaoh's snakes,
stiffening again then into a staff, in Sinai
(Africa's ear), struck an improbable rock.

Crown

"And God said, Let there be lights in the firmament of the heaven to divide the day from the night; and let them be for signs, and for seasons, and for days, and years."
(Gen. 1:14)

Advent

How can the wolf not kill the lamb?
How can the rich be any less
Than in my heart I think I am?
What wars are won with gentleness?
How can the lamb trust and not die?
How can the poor be any more
Exalted by the King than I
Am cleaning his house and holding his door?
I'll take my sweet time, then, and make
My own hands' best work the place
That's safest, best, for my Lord's sake.
Faith's not an entrance singing grace.
So I, unbroken, still defy
His mild child till mute stones must cry.

Christmas

Visceral house, dark warmth, whose waters float
A sealed boat, ark of grace, containing all
Oceans inside you, through you the Word wrote
Us and you, who in your flesh bore light. Call
Dark night day, then, so sin, too, can sink
Buried with death, which these fresh waters drown
Better than years or ink. Blot out night, drink
Forgiveness; the child's hand, mouth, writes you down.

Unconquered Son, your church has made this day
That you made, from *Mithras*, *Sol Invictus*,
Elah-Gabal, not, though, from the same clay
we share or washed old hopes but a chaste rashness.
Eternity sleeps on the old year's bier
As the still word speaks that we might hear.

Ordinary Time

Green season, wreath of Sundays, each a feast
Woven with years to lift new crowns of praise
Without delay, we leave the wise men east
Again, amazed, until we take highways
Of fire, confused to understand, schooldays,
His pupils teaching, foreigners come home,
That as we walk through his green wood's new maze
Again, we're set at sea, and with Him, roam
Freely to find his ways our own and us
More ours in this, and his; his heart-sighs comb
Wheat with the sun's wind to make us lustrous.
We rise in his death, with his breath our compass.
We kneel to stand. We run. We discover
A life mysteriously familiar.

Lent

Tempered by hope, bright sadness, forty-day exile,
I fear I grow too happy in unhappiness,
Mastering myself (as if I could) through new denial
To set an idol up, false cross, and lose God's goodness.
Oh let me not, encumbered, stumble the long mile
Back the wrong way. And let my heart not love you less,
For this, sweet Jesus, that you antedate my trial

And my denial. (How could I take what you possess?)
You give your good gifts, and I lose all my merit.
How do I confess this last, worst, fear: your church sins,
And I in it. I wear Cain's mark and inherit
Silence, damnation's profit, and your old foe wins.
O God, forbid it! Must Death's laugh trump love's brilliance,
Rock of All Mirth, and the tomb swallow deliverance?

Easter

Year's pivot, new day, here the whole year swings
Open forever through spring's first full moon,
Blood-stained posts, death's angel, and night's noon:
Christ's fire our door. Cut Isaac's fastenings!
Through the Red Sea, Egypt's slavery, God brings
His people home, so always now he will soon
Flower in orchards, bear his new fruit, and prune
The dead branches while risen Israel sings.
So that we might live truth, be our new life
That we might live; and living, give us joy
To live your peace, your joyous peace that gives
Joy to the stranger, joy that kills all strife
And pride, your joy that death cannot destroy,
Such joy your love, love's risen joy that lives.

Whitsunday

New feast of weeks, new day of God's first fruits,
Heat, wind, and tongues: confusion rains down fire.
What can this mean? Nothing is as it seems.
You might as well tear up the tree by its roots
As mix us up like this! Call me a liar
Then, and set me on fire! I understand

Joel called what's true God's truth. Still, my worst dreams
Smile, calling me brother, and no one suits
Me like my own, though Peter's sights go higher.
David foresaw what this confusion means.
He is alive. Turned out, I think I meet,
Empty and hot, thirsty, and understood,
Him here in his city, turning to greet
Me freer than my own presumption would.

Feast of Christ the King

King of Glory, humiliation's crown,
Reigns from on high; the thief beside him sees
What others can't; and when they take him down,
Mary can see, not touch, God's mysteries,
And may I kneel, now, taste, and see what he
Gave to release me to freely return
Love as his gift in perfect liberty
Serving the King whose saints like near stars burn.
Diadems of his holiness and grace,
His living truth is justice, love, and peace,
A clear spring flowing from that holy place
Where laborers rest, knowing their release.
See, know, taste his goodness. He who was least
Offers himself in love, each day a feast.

Holy Conversation
(Vittore Carpaccio)

"The saints in conversation!"
She tells her husband across the small room
Though alone myself I'd thought talk,
The interchange of touch or look,
Or music's sound, or soundless print, the loom
And shuttlecock's motion,

The counterweighted bucket
Lifting more easily the well water
For the hermit, his grotto cut
In a skull's shape, might mean rather
I see my eye might thread the needle's eye
Of the world and reply

To arch on arch, lion
In his master's solitary labor
Complicit, grateful, awaken
To flimsy clay fording over
A clot of roots and trees beginning to leaf
Over what's just enough

Bridge to suffice and step
Across what's there in this picture, a boy
With arms like water throwing seeds;—
Then, that peak's eye: two black dots slap
A smaller third dot, infinity's toy,
Which, where work fails, succeeds.

Employment

Why is a life not like a day?
The fruit trees flower. The clematis
        Opening a pink spray
Of gold centers like the wild rose
        Was made for this
Torrent of color. One lost bee
        Taps my windows
From inside before it flies free

Through blue the same bird welcomes
Each dawn's first fresh moments before
        Invisible flight comes
To me wondering where it's flown:
        From this near shore
To the boar's next hill—or the woods—
        Where some unknown
Spikes pierce through moss their paper hoods?

Bright mornings, cold useless use,
What good is there in this
        Urge I must feel to lose
My life in a fruitless push?
        A gold bomb's miss
Tripped in the tree in front of me
        Drops in a rush,
Wheels, white song's scythe, stone floor, grass sea.

from **RIB CAGE** (2001)

Little Town

A little rain spits in the open tent,
the auctioneer ringing small bits of meaning
against his more meaningless bits of singing.
Heavy Victorian pieces—inlaid secretaries
with accordion lids that wink shut through grooves,
marble-topped servers, lyre tables
with full wings let down for room—
float on long sheets of plywood that move as you walk
over the sucking mud-mess at their base.

Most of the family shops in town
don't open at all anymore.

Old pistols, silver, china, beds, clocks, desks;
some fluted rose chimneys for Viennese gaslights;
clocks in the Empire Style, with gilded Titans
reclining to turn towards time's face;
rice beds that rise so far
from the ground that small children
might sleep in them only
at their peril; thimbles,
pewter pitchers, velour
mahogany boxes for silver settings.

The house behind the auction is Federal style.
In the 1820s, when it was built,
the whole town was new, ripped
from the forest
at the edge of the Barrens.

Some Amish families,
having moved a community here
a few decades ago
from Ohio, mingle with the world.
The muddy barefoot boys
in buttoned denim—
they're all grins.

In a shed by the tent, I walk into another
auction: "arrowheads"
in a shoebox, collected
on somebody's farm.

A bonneted woman in her fifties,
her daughter's hand in hers, both of them
in black and white, hovers,
tired, in the dark,
her free arm resting on another
child on its way. The floating body
of the world takes and lives.

At the Window

White calla lilies gathering like flocks,
Gold tongues extended to the glozing sun
Outside her kitchen window, she can see
Beyond them, in a field of Queen Anne's lace,

Her husband, son, and daughter, soapy water
Splashing up from the pressure cooker lid
Catching her in the corner of one eye
As steam rises from the still running rinse.

Starting to cry almost against herself,
She turns to the porcelain angels on the wall,
Each one a wooden step above the next
On a wooden emblem of the crescent moon.

But why should she cry now, she asks herself,
The cancer thriving in her small son's head
Removed, the worst of the danger past?
The redbuds burst like barnacles from the bark.

Intercessor

He prayed for weeks, till praying grew routine.
He prayed for healing, and his prayers' keen
Insistence brought him sometimes to his knees
As in his mind's eye, images, like bees

From the shook hive, flew. Whom had prayer healed,
Protected? Whom could he, unshielded, shield?
But still he felt compelled: he held to hope
Though when it slipped, it burned him like a rope.

He would do better. He had better sense
Than to be cast aside with no defense.
He sought out Jesus, thinking that he could
Take up the matter: what he got was blood,

Lulled bees, an empty tomb, grape hyacinths,
As walking through the borough's labyrinths,
Holding his sister, thankless healing light
Together in his head, he fought to fight.

River

Old Reverend Miller stopped to talk to me
By Lincoln's cabin, the memorial
A temple on a hill with granite steps
That children, mailing pennies, paid for, near
The sinkhole where the Lincolns cooled their food
And, drawing water, may have stood to look
Into the pool that flows below to feed,
Through limestone honeycombs, another spring.

Some days the stillness felt a spectacle:
The columns' fluted, bone-white symmetry,
Pin oaks, twelve other species, each one oak,
Red cedars, dogwoods, poplars, the blue shade,
The red bird's call a thick drop in the pool
Over the golden floor, the flick of red
Within the mind, an echoing of lines,
Until more children's voices filled the room.

Casually he let slip the story how
His father, just a baby, came to know
The inside of a jail, his mother, white,
Having been put there just as soon as she
Gave birth to him, how, soon as it was seen
The father wasn't white, could not be white,
("miscegenation" defining them the crime)
She was, with her transgression, jailed, cast out—

Both child and mother, once unjailed, unmoored
And left to shift alone in times before
Women could find their food or livelihood
Without their men folk, when a marriage made
Across the races bound no man nor wife
And crossed the law, as well, no children made
Legitimate or heir to what might pass
From parent to child, no law to shape their place

For them except in placelessness, and then
This minister whose family name I share,
A name so wide and large whole families
Swim in the dual confluences it makes
On both sides of the town, both black and white,
Left me with that, no other purpose than,
I guess, to turn me towards the river's course,
Bearing some sense within of where it's been.

Free Fall

She hears he's died. "Thank God," she thinks at first.
Then wants to punch something or someone, break
A wall or face, then stops, collects herself.

Rehearsals—Mozart's *Requiem*—become
Where she imagines endless distances
He cannot measure, and through which he falls

(He neither learns, nor understands, nor changes)
Until, with time, some several months, the hard
Working through runs (those fugal permutations!),

She finds she offers up for him a prayer,
Thinking him small, a pitiable man,
Finding she can, now, get some sleep and not

Wake as her body tightens, jerking her
From the mattress high enough to feel the weight
Of falling back to earth and not to rest.

Move On

Looking at me as if out of a well,
She tells me there is nothing good in her life
To write about, so she has to write about Jesus.
She has the look of an animal used to being beaten,
Trusting nothing but the swift stick of grace,
Truth's only true sign.
                                        Father Augustine
Struggles for the raptures of our silences
Into and out of which everything is always
Falling, binding and unbinding within us
Like the whir of the June bug under the pin
Of the probing scientist suddenly gone silent.
It is as if the small lights of the intellect
Dancing at night in the fields, random
And constantly shifting, moved in parody
Of the fixed stars of heaven. It is not so.
The stretched skins of the scriptures keep us cool
In our journey through Babylon and Egypt.
We must pack up our tents with the ark
And in the cool light of the evening move on.

Mystery Cycle
(*in memoriam* Mark, Richard, Don, Bob, Henry)

I

As useless as the wind, less spirited
Than those whom you have disinherited,
Can you forgive my sin against the spirit?
More to the point, can I believe you hear it?
The deathbed watch, the morphine, the few words
Mark's mind was clear enough to struggle towards
Enabled him to say what he must say
Before he fell asleep and turned away.
His lover left Mark's voice on the machine,
Then turned it off and left the phone to ring.

II
(Easter)
Bright brass rings out, and little girls with daisies
Traverse the aisles with fistfuls of his praises
In deference to the love that still moves me
Like Thomas toward that known anatomy.

III
Hoping to heal myself, I worked with children,
Believing heaven promises a haven.
Carrying watercolors from the sink,
Distracted, I stepped on an I-V link,
Feeling the valve break. She started to bleed
Before the attending nurse could intercede.
That night I finished working on my car.
The red gunk stuck to my hands like tar.

IV
The girl with the cross on her forehead screams,
The cross measuring the radiation's beams.
She will not be consoled while someone not
Her mother takes her in her arms to rock
And keeps on rocking though she doesn't stop;
A father holding his son to lift him up
From his uneasy breathing for a bath
Imagines how each breath must feel like wrath
Against which, helplessly, he goes through motions—
Particular, exacting ministrations.

V
Visionary fragments fall
Around me at the funeral:
Asperges, sprinkling with wet cedar,
A dancer dancing at the altar,
All Easter white, appointed scriptures,
The table spread with childhood pictures.
Remembering how we each were cast,
How he played Satan, I played Christ,
How my raised hand could send him back
When he came at me with an ax,
Everywhere in our common fiction
I meet affection as affliction.
I think our dead friends ring us round:
Beelzebub, the lesser fiend
Who donned a checkered table napkin
And robes to play a Turkish sultan.
And Pilate mumbling from the altar
For Jesus's crucifixion. Water
Rang in a metal salad bowl.
I played my pre-appointed role
And stepped, the still word, from the tomb,

The concrete cold, my bare feet numb.
"The strife is o'er, the battle won."
(I couldn't die for anyone.)
The guards stopped playing cards and rose
Supposedly in mute surprise.
Wrapped in burlap, Henry struck
The bare floor with his pike. It spoke.

No Stars

I
My friends around the table toast my time
Spent, and the time to come. And those not here,
Where I will someday be, may they drink wine
As good as this, eat berries near as sweet
With cream as fresh. And may there be no end
To such receptions, windows throwing back
Neither the window's backing nor night's blackness,
But such light candles find in human faces.

II
An eagle, diving, breaks the Bay to lift
A silver, heavy fish, climbing with it
As when one stands too quickly and the head,
Flushed with its blood, believes no stars it sees,
Becomes the ringing in the ears, and knows
The children's voices, echoing, declaim
The day a bowl of light and the blood's dome
Commingled light and lightness, bowl and blue.

III
I am the passenger the pilot lifts
To be slapped back and rattled till we sit
Stable between low clouds and high. The roar,
My bones, are one. We fly to dawn, the Rose
Empyrean where my friend piloted
His pain that maimed him through the love he bore
Yet did not maim his love, though he grew weak,
That love might bear him and no pain remain.

Iron Brine

She looked at him to say her kidneys might
Never work right. What she had done, she could
Not change. Her body might not heal itself.
Her eyes, he noticed, registered surprise.

A whole communal household hadn't kept
Her from herself, from what she'd planned to do.
It didn't matter that they called the cops.
It didn't matter that they took her keys
And sat on her until policemen came,
Sat on her screaming, fighting to get free,
To lock her in the ward for two whole days,
The legal limit, though she'd said she'd kill
Herself, she'd drive to the Golden Gate and jump.

Rat poison: plastic packets in the closet.
While cleaning up the mess, he thought of glands.

She cut the packets open and ate them.

He helped to talk her into going back.
He drove her with her boyfriend to the place
From which she had escaped late in the night.

She stripped her bed and hanged herself with sheets
Where cameras couldn't see her, in the shower.

She broke out.
                    She committed herself.
Last night, a New Year's caller asked him had
They known, before his friend's death, what she'd do.

A quaver in her voice alerted him.
They kept on talking till her voice grew calm.

He dreamed of lying belly-down in a ditch.
He saw a rattler rasp around a corner
And watched its smooth, pearly pink jaw unhinge
To strike him in the eye.
                                        He prays for her,
That she not tease the asp, that she not play
That part that Cleopatra played, and sleeps
Fitfully through the long night by the phone.

*

Where does the house of the heart begin
And everything else end?

With time, she learned
A necessary being in and out,
Detachment from, engagement with, her life,
Seeing herself, third-person, even—more
Open, at least, to things as they might be—
Feeling less fated—free, with possibilities.

*

The New Year's caller started making changes.
She even learned to dive hundreds of miles
From any ocean so she could, once there,
Begin exploring reefs and sunken wrecks.
She felt something inside her turn her out.
Her dive instructor grew impatient with her.
She wasn't paying close enough attention.
She followed a school of fish away from him.

Swirling within a school of swirling fish,
She was encircled by a six-foot eel
As it swam past her. Though the thought of it
Horrified the caller, she insisted that
She loved it. He imagined, though he'd never
Seen one, eyes and mouth uplifted like
A guppy's, undersides billowing like
Sidewinders moving over sand around
Her, utterly liquid, then off someplace else,
As in her natural element, she swims
The world's warm iron brine, light's curtain in
Its fall illumined with the sun's full fire.

Garden

I
Sod ripping like fabric
Under the lip of my shovel,
Stacked and moved to the worked-up
Bald spots of the center of the yard,
I envision the border bed yet to be
Pitched-fork deep, topsoil
To be mixed with the ubiquitous
Roots of the sweet gum
So old and broad and high
It's embroiled itself
In practically everything living,
Compost to be mixed with the red clay
That will dye my clothes
Iron red and not be washed out,
Bone meal and blood meal
To stir with this little steel claw.

II
A neighbor cut his brittle hackberry
That will no longer let fall the heavy
Parts of itself
Pell-mell, dangerously, when least expected
So now there's a little corner of full sun
For my old rose.

I picked its dried leaves,
Pruned the branches,
Pruning again as
They blackened.

My faith will be water.

III
Cuttings, starters,
Bulbs, and seeds
From my mother's garden:

Purple-leafed
Canna lilies (I put out no poisons
And so some of the leaves
Must be made lace)
That will bloom red and mottled orange
Just as they bloom
In her mother's garden,
Banty roosters
Strutting midnight's rainbows.

A thorny quince whose red
Will ache in early April.

Black-eyed Susans:
Clenched anemones.

Goats' beards:
Little sticks
That root a year
Before swelling
Native hoariness.

One hydrangea
Holding its globes.

Broken Consort

The soprano lawyer,
Student of Balinese
Theater, who has saved the dead
From a carver who sells
But will not carve tombstones—

The depressive whose
Ballast of meds holds
Upright his boat,
Intimate of
Interstellar spaces—

The widower shuffling
Anxiously, determinedly
Beside me
In the processional
To find his place—

The healer whose
Beeper draws him
When not
Expected from our
Circle of sound

Stand around
The piano to make
A semicircle
Under the carved
Wooden altar

To hear each other
Better *a cappella* and so
Keep in pitch and give
The shifting lead
Line its due prominence,

Singing Brahms
Who seems to me
Now more like Bach
Than Bach himself even,
Though yet still Brahms

Writing as if
For a keyboard instrument,
Not these voices
(inexact, no matter
The training or timbre)

Breaking repetition and
Variation, praise echoing
Shaped praise,
Making me feel whole, held
In how I'm not.

Ark

(for Betsy and Gail)

The chuppah's quilted
Blues and purples, stars
Held by the world's four
Corners, make them one

Less than this living
Liquidly they do
Together, sailboat
On the lake, day's work

Over, or nearly
Over, dinner's mess
Yet to be scrubbed up,
Legislature out

Of session, no new
Lobbying to do,
The working poor not
Left yet in the cold

By men with money,
The day's phone calls made,
New signings scheduled
Up and down the coasts

For books she chose as
Publicist so hope
Might make a living
In our midst somehow.

When the week's work is
Done two women sing
Their *shabbos* prayers,
Light cupped in their hands.

Magic Flute

Following his song's lead,
each held stop speaks,
past the lightness of speech, the need
for what song lacks
and seeks,

slackening its soft cries
through the black trees
where the black velvet table lies—
ripe fruit, the blaze
of ease

on silver bowls and plates
—want's clean, cold glow—
while Papageno contemplates
his master's law,
to know

how not to eat the fruit
or drink the wine.
With his cage of reeds and new flute
flung with his fine
light chain

of bells over his arm—
magic, the full
song of the bird-catcher—no harm,
no pentateuchal
purr, pull

of night or night's sightless
adamantine
center will leave him any less
free from this pain,
the shine

of light through the film's frames,
the theatre
of faces silver, all time's aims
seared through like fear
with care,

like the song of Daphnis,
the Great Shepherd,
lost in his high noontime likeness,
caught, with each chord,
each word,

freely in love's low door.
Intensely white—
her hand lightly in his before
Death's Angel's late,
long flight—

the transfiguring wing
touches the couple.
Then they move slowly through the ring,
the jingle-jangle,
the pull

of lightness leading past
the fire's force,
through the Magician's test, his last
ordeal, his curse
the source

of sweet oblivion
not death, his art
to see how he can harden
love's healing hurt,
the heart.

Prothalamion

1

While crickets sing like small chinks in a chain,
two friends sit in a room with corniced windows
opening on a maple and the cool
night air, one reading to the other one
a poem about a reader in a room
alone and reading to himself, his light
the only light. Each voice takes turns to make
the sound of the story as it should be,
turning it over on his tongue to turn
his listener back against what he had heard
first, when he first heard what had to be told,
as if to see which pleased the other more.

2
Rehearsal

I take the steps up: the eagle, Saint Paul
above the spiral. High, I read
Paul's hymn,
love's scrim
of letters, then, instead
of walking, fall
down the smooth stone
stairs as I'm thrown
free through the air
to look up at the bridesmaids, their bright hair,

penumbral blue blooms and forget-me-nots
over me, the three stunned Graces

cooing,
a ring
arranging its faces,
its triune knots
free, garland-like
while voices strike
—water on water—
the thunder of gently swelling laughter.

3
A Gift

A basket
made from cut vines:
I have not cut them or gathered them.
It is strong.
It can hold many things.
It does not smell like honeysuckle flowers
though woven with honeysuckle vines.

4
Song of Songs

Camphire, saffron scents—
cedar beams, rafters of fir:
let day
and the air in
the room where time has been.

5

Where time and time's strands splice:
the soul depicts itself a paradise.

6

I fall into the waters of myself
and cannot rise. Great boulders rim the pool
on Stony Creek, the April water cold
from melting snow, new rain, the memory
of winter sleeping in the dense bedrock.
You jump in and I can see clean through to
the stones like coins in your now smaller hand
before you push off and shoot up thirty feet
to the clear surface through the slow blue trout.
Breaking the calm water, you holler out
how it is so cold it makes your heart stop,
how I should try it, how I should jump in too.
Montaigne and Etienne de la Boétie
effaced the seam that joined them with a song
that took a lifetime in the singing. Asked
how such a friendship came to be, one said,
"because it was he, because it was I."
It's morning, the pungent alien smell
of wet leaves rising. Awake last night,
I sang to myself with the kind of song
that the seven-year-locusts sing to leave
their amber paper shells hung in the trees.

from **IRON WHEEL** (1998)

Words

Let the ploughman till the dark earth of the heart
turning it over, rich with worms, white grubs, roots.
Let the blinkered mule cut the sheets of sod
steaming over into the sunlight, for the earth must hurt
with blackbirds peppering it in the wake of the blade.

My father once saw land he had appraised
for the state, a cemetery, dug up for a new road.
The diggers wore gloves and masks to protect them
from cholera and dysentery. He said they didn't find anything
but dirt a little lighter than what was around it—
and here and there a blue button or a buckle.

Elvira told the Presbytery: "If I was to know
my son was queer, I'd wish him dead
to his face." And Paul, passing
his sister with the woman she'd lived with
for five years: "I don't know and I don't want
to know."
        The Rolling Fork Baptist Church,
Kentucky County, Commonwealth of Virginia,
set this question before the Salem Association (1789):
"*Quare*, Is it lawful for a member of Christ's
Church to keep his fellow creatures in perpetual slavery?"
The question, "in accordance with scripture," was answered
in the affirmative, so Rolling Fork Baptist Church
withdrew.
        Severns Valley Baptist Church, 1796:
"*Quare*, Is slavery oppression or not? It is oppression."

And I think about you, John, the youngest
river-rat brother in the yellowing picture.
One I love stands beside you, his arm over your wet shoulder.
Your parents found you in the garage one afternoon
after school with the door closed and the car running.
Those who love you have only their loss
for words, their unanswerable need for speech
lingering like a button or a deep black bruise.

Stroke

For months she could not speak,
Breathing forced through a trache—
Tubes, lines she tried to pull
Out or break.

For hours I read to her
Newspapers, stories I chose.
Convinced she couldn't hear
Any of those

I read a poem by Frost:
"Drink and be whole again
Beyond confusion." I
Saw her reach then

With one arm for the book
That she grasped and held close
To her chest, weeping. Words
Meant to give took.

The Dresses

She falls, feeling her head bounce like a ball
On the red linoleum floor,
Not feeling anything, her eyes
Wide open. Minutes later, or days
For all she knows or cares, she gets up
Beginning to remember what she saw
When she wasn't seeing anything at all—
The flies ping pinging on the screen door,
The constantly irresolute white wall,
The clock, with its rays, beating on the wall.
She goes to town and buys herself a dress,
Though her children will have to do without,
Living on dandelion salads and bread,
Whatever animals her sons can catch
In their baited boxes by the creek.
But nothing's really good enough to keep.
She goes with the hurt that takes her where she breathes,
Picking her up like a lover till she faints
Over and over, bruising herself before
The face that tells her that she's worthless
—God the father or her father the god—
That rush of emptiness the only way
At least not to be beaten in the face.
She keeps on buying and falling until
She feels justified in her beautiful dresses,
Paying for them, dearly, until she can't
Stand up anymore at all and she's sent
To Our Lady of Peace where she's shocked
Out of oblivions and what's she's been.

Perspective

At the apex of the gray gravel tar-shingled roof,
Having hurled his chest against a bright day's accumulated warmth,
Chafing first he elbows and then on all fours
Making his way up the steep incline,
King now of his heap: a neighbor's truck
On cinder blocks, the Salt River's silver reeds
In the hollow between the Knobs,
Grackles whirring like gears and springs in the near oak,
No machinery of hope, God's great ticker
Apostrophizing him, broken bloody heap in gravel.

To see himself as such stanches his heart's wound.
Salvation comes to him for that necessary second
In not being himself, in seeing himself
As if from a serene distance so that he doesn't jump.

*

To be in a high room loved deeply for what he is not
Fills him with the need suddenly to jump over everyone,
Out the glass, through the window, and away.
He can't breathe. He needs desperately to be
Able to breathe. "But I'm not that, either,"
He thinks. He is like a sparrow he saw once
Trapped in the back room of the barn against the window
Battering itself against what it couldn't see
To get away from the hands that wanted to catch it
And set it free. He is on the brink
And must eventually turn around or fly through.
The question, though, is how and where to.
Some days getting out seems all that matters.

The neck of the starved winged thing that sings snapped.
It lies stiffening on the oily burlap sack beneath the window.
If only it had let itself be held, cradled
In cupped hands, taken to the door, and let go.

Iron Wheel

Wearing his aviator's cap in early Indian summer,
Hunched on his flipped-over pail,
He knows and doesn't know me.
He knows and doesn't know himself,
Bombardier in wire spectacles,
Red bandana slipped over his spectacles and tied
To keep dirt and dust out of the hole
His pocketed glass eye has left.

It's the cobs themselves he wants, not their hard seed
Which he lets fall on the concrete floor in a pile.
He says that they make the winter's best kindling,
And kindling is what he needs in the cold.
His frame is spare. He looks as thin as a girl.
His daughter swears no heart's more tender.

He lay stretched out asleep on the couch by closed curtains
In his bedroom last time I came to look for him.
Light in the room clung to his face as to white stone.
His thinness let show another man's bone.
And that pallor on his face was the face of his father,
The father he forgave as he sat by his deathbed
To which he took me as a boy so I could meet him,
Where he blinked at me, spoke, and turned away.
My grandfather's brothers and sisters thought he must be mad.
Of all of them, he had the most to forgive, and he forgave.

With the stub of a thumb and his palm's hard heal
He squats on the pail and kneads the ends of an ear bare.
The cast-iron wheel with thick waved spokes
And the little knob by which he works

The magnificent antique grinder
Turn as he drops in an ear so that gears can tear
Kernels from the cob, spitting out kernels and cobs
In different places at different ends of the wood box
In the center of which the wheel hangs square.

Original Sin

The boy bounced through the barn, having his way
over beast and fowl. The cattle, heads in stocks,
fed quietly on grain while milkers sucked
at those old teats, catching the milk in cans
sealed against the open world's infections.
The boy would pet those fettered heads, though they
lowed, fearing the alien hand. Partly to divert
the boy, in part to feed his mouser's new
young litter, the man took hold of one fat teat
with one hand while another grabbed the lump
of bony fur. A stream of white steamed high
—in midair—to the open mouth; that small
thing, squirming in the hand that fed it,
hung by its head, the four paws whirling free.
The boy was not to touch these. Feral cats,
to live, could never come to know the need
for human touch. These kittens came to be
the apple in his Eden, the one bad fruit.
He stalked them daily, no one seeing him,
until he caught the long-haired, coal-gray one
and held it in his coat till it grew warm.
He felt its warmth against his body, felt,
as well, the purring he had hoped to earn.
He walked out on the frost-encrusted mud,
that small life burrowed next to him, not
even seeing the great dog that would knock
him down, knowing nothing of those expert jaws
that snapped the delicate stem of the neck
that rolled and coughed up blood, the kitten's eyes
darkening in his hands. He cried and cried
and not a word was said could change it.

Story
(Freud's Fable)

She strikes him as she's learned love has to strike
to make him hers, marking him with her own
marks over again, the vessel she pours
all of her old lost love back into
to make the water wine, the kind of sign
the boy learns to spell back when she reads him
how Job, his children all dead, cut himself
with the sharp shards of the broken pots,
which stood, each shard, for a wife or child he'd lost.
And while she holds him, rocking him to sleep,
the outline of election stinging his cheek,
her sweet voice singing him through all harm's way,
singing his name, and her name, he can feel,
like love's true rage, that dark wine darkening him,
another picture on another page—
the ram's curved crown hung in the tangled branches,
through the bushes that mad eye seeking him out.

Intensive Care Waiting Room

The heart, kidneys and liver of the eleven-year-old
had begun to fail when he was camping—then began

disintegrating. His mother watched herself
being interviewed, nightly, on the TV in Intensive Care.

People across the state must have been eating dinner,
coming in from the fields for ham, cut tomatoes, creamed corn,

or out of their cars after the commute across the river
to Indiana—or in Okolona or Lexington—

getting in from GE, the Ford Plant, or the races,
and thinking about the "poor woman,"

perhaps even feeling genuine concern for her troubles—
one day a packet of letters scrawled

by a class of third graders in a town in Pennsylvania
which she cradles in her hands like a precious weight—

or faint delight in and horror at
how what had happened was so utterly random.

*

I could find no other reason for the *National Enquirer*,
the only "reading matter" other than the Gideon Bible,

both of which I, for one, begin to read with relish.
And what does it mean when the prim lady in her sixties,

the volunteer in a pink uniform, officiously, joylessly,
with the look of a late medieval Florentine saint,

distributes coffee, pointing to "reading matter"? I think
of gray matter and then consider that the participal

or adjectival form makes it seem that it's the matter
that does the reading, so to speak, that *it*

reads *us*, that I, in this strange room,
am brought into being by the sex life

of Lucille Ball, or the child carried dead in the womb
of an eighty-year-old woman, the Annunciation or Hannah.

*

After Dr. Gray gave the boy a new heart he sewed a piece
of artificial matter to replace a valve in my mother's heart

that had been punctured by a small fragment of bone
which had flown from her rib. When I got to the waiting room

from California, my father had just thrown a washrag
through the ceiling, for she had lived, surviving

the helicopter lift and the operation, neither of which
she had been given much hope of a chance of surviving.

*

Some nights I was kept up by a woman I've since come to call
the Tiger Lady, who came in a tight tiger-skin dress,

fat, in her fifties, to talk about chasing her ex-husband
with a butcher knife, the same story over and over,
as if to convince herself that she really did it,

weaving herself into the fearless story she told herself
in the dark, waiting, from three to five in the morning.

*

I sit up and read the psalms all night
and am, in a sense, comforted. And in I Kings:

"but the LORD was not in the fire, and after
the fire a still small voice." At four o'clock a family
runs screaming through the waiting room. My sister,

a trooper, looks up and turns over; my little brother
downstairs getting coffee; my father, for once, sleeping.

*

Reverend Livingstone, with his fifties gray felt hat,
white ivory cross, hovers over his retarded daughter

in the room across—she is drowning—my grandparents
holding my mother's hand. Someone wheels a body in a black bag

past us so I close the door. "What's wrong?" I say
we can't go yet and we all just stand there.

*

On Easter I make it to church.
The altar floats with dogwood

crowns of green stamens
a great white sheet
he is risen! he is risen!
forsythia breaking on the sidewalk
the rose rising through its blues
through red clay bricks
the broad brown back
of the Ohio
rippling past bridges
sun playing on the foam
sun in the windows
blue and red and gold,
and in a side chapel
Mary in enfolding black,
gold needles encircling her face, gold
floating on the bordered lace.
I feel like kneeling
stumbling out into
the disorienting light.

*

A friend of my mother's, well-meaning, told her
to be comforted, for nothing happens without God's will.

Though she remembered little else, she remembered that,
a feeling she said like a cold knife shivering through her.

*

The people in the room were held by a bond, wordlessly broken
when the loved one died or got better and was wheeled away,

the place becoming a past for those leaving,
a fictional history made real by a future

that rearranged what had been into what had to have been
or, for those free from the usual piety, what just happened.

*

God-forsaken, telling, getting told, the tale
takes off and takes us, my God at the center

of his own God-forsakenness, the heart
which has to be other than what it is.

Ariadne
(for Noël Florence)

1

Your kitten's grown like a weed this week.
(You named her for a goddess left on Naxos.)
Just now, I walked into your empty room—
carnations in one corner, two weeks old.
I have a picture of you looking like
the goddess that you played, the one you said
you hated, sometimes thinking you were her,
not you.
       Three o'clock. There's no sound out,
and what I think I'm dreaming is true life.
Your mother's wandering the halls, and you're
nowhere. Wine bottle candles through the house
make up this vigil she's afraid to break.
She's leaving little gifts—piles at our doors—
the sort of things we can remember by—
a wooden rabbit, posters, clothes, your books.

2

I run through January's early spring—
acacia blossoming its fuzzy suns
that hang grapelike, abundant, in vast bunches—
a golden Grecian light made geometric,
angled through the houses, interspersing
low, near sunset, through the mingled leaves.
Huge eucalyptus rush with water sounds
into the beds of breezes. Nothing moves
of its own will. The under-eyes of leaves
flash gilded silver. Orchard grass, in tufts,
glows inwardly with early yellow light,

a winter green that grows back what it lost.
The fire trail takes off, but I stay put.
Below, the bay burns. One small boat
careens into the blinding spot, is lost
for a few blinks, is visible again
smack in the center, leaving a slug's track—
the kind that makes a different liquid light
on concrete walks, along the flower bed.

3

Your father putters helplessly at things.
I held you crying, feeling your thin frame—
girlish, the woven wicker of your ribs.
We feel the pain in waves. You've left us all
by choice. We're each cut off in midsentence.
When morning comes, your mother shows the wound
a misplaced candle burned into a beam—
the beam that runs the length of the whole house.

Revival
(for Melinda Cheryl Fox)

1

In your green low-shouldered gown
you step out of the black,
the side of your face black
where the car struck
snapping you into the air.
Where have you gone?
When will I not feel
the hovering pull
like the light
shivering of skin when
hair passes dry wool?
Bruised, speechless, you go back
through my revolving door.
I take the bread, the wine,
the cross passing.
It is Good Friday
and I am singing
because it is good
to say I love, I hurt,
good to be able
to say that it is not
fair, and that God knows this.

2

We drove to Louisville. The shopping mall
was empty except for people like us

going to see movies. What it was we saw
I can't remember. But you were trembling
and when I asked why you told me how
Marsha's car had flipped into a ditch.
You were so nervous that you kept fiddling
with the black brochure the usher had given you
so that when the show was over your face
was black. You giggled—nervous, embarrassed,
your neck flushed red.
                              Your brother died in May.
I remember him in the back of the class,
his head shaved, his eyes sunk in black sockets.
Your mother kept his room intact and talked
about him as if he had never died.
That summer we drove around in my Catalina,
the air wet with fresh-cut hay and sweet,
the blur of tinny things in the moonlight
flashing nowhere but on the edge of vision.
You talked about him too, but without
the distances of self-regarding grief.
You loved him, though you hadn't always been good
to each other. He had hit you once
with a hoe when you were a little girl.

That Christmas we went to Gethsemane,
the monks' tombstones in the cemetery,
inscribed in French and Latin, irrelevant
to the well-dressed people on their way
to the high white nave. The candles and voices
became desire, the Word's fierce longing
to take on flesh spreading out like a flower.
The night you died I was with another,
a guy I loved much as I loved you,
no lover, but "too close." I want to touch

your hair, your bruised face, to make it better.
You brother comes to hit me with my hoe,
but after years of letting him hit me,
wanting him to, feeling the blade's sharp shock,
welcoming it, I wrench the smooth wood
out of his hand and turn to touch your face.

3
Revival

Everyone singing, an enthusiasm
no bacchanalian revelry could rival.
It's late spring, the sap has started rising.
They've brought a bunch of preachers in to preach.
And in the front, the oracle, the mike
passes from hand to hand in slow progression.
(Such are the rites of true confession.)

Sometimes the people are the sin they're saying
—lust, avarice, jealousy, hate, despair—
until passion's utter obliteration
wears away each soiled particular
leaving the people to walk out not weeping.

Fire Flowers

I

Sometimes when you're
talking to me, your voice
goes soft, or so it feels
to me, and slips,
like slug silk on skin,
between my innermost
parts. (I would not
otherwise
have known them.)

And then you are
no longer talking
to me or are talking
in another voice or
I realize that your
gentleness has nothing
to do with me
in particular
and I stand
amazed humming
like rubbed crystal.

II

You once told me what we
desire is what we are.

You run, bounding
over the breakwater's

irregular boulders
to the second lighthouse
where you sing
"Rejoice! Rejoice!"
full-throated
in your natural register
as the sun drops a moment
between the twin opacities
of cloud bank and ocean.

Do we "dwell
in lowly exile here"?

Or is this Jerusalem?

III

Enameled apocalypse,
both veil and the ripped veil—

all that is seared
through, unsoiled,
sits in hesitant hands—
light gravel,
ash under the nails.

In the marsh grasses
your lover's ashes mix,
in needle-thin schools,
with the ice and the salt,
and the gullets of gulls.

IV

The heart's meadows bloom
a communal gold
haze in a green room
of cold, short days.

Longing's sent up new
shoots, forced narcissus.
Who would not smell this
obvious odor?

I can give no gift equal
to the gift not to be ungiven,
to the gift given without intention,
the gift not meant to be given.

V

I haven't said yet what
I meant, or at least
what I set out
to say, so I'll try.

I stooped through love's
low door alone. Heart,
mind, and body knew
each other as if for
the first time and grew

like one field burned
back—new leaves, blue
lupine, gold globe
mallow, against the
rain-brightened black.

Here is what I meant
to do: to gather up some
few blooms for you
in well-wishing and
be on my way
other than who I was.

From the Museum

Rooting in brittle mortar—
gypsum plaster, sand, and water—
bougainvillea grew around the arches,
in walls, and through the fences of the town,
the one old woman in the town museum
opening a window in the spiral
staircase overlooking a river
and its alluvial leavings:
green, yellow-green, and brown rectangular
and polygonal plots along the river
beyond the town walls built, so the signs say,
by Charlemagne's son, where the Allies
bombed and flattened houses that have since
not needed to be rebuilt,
the old woman remembering some of the dead
by name.
        She notices someone
descending past the family of farmers
and the town walls towards
a lacquered wagon of blue and red
interweaving vines, rising smoke,
and beyond this, in a clearing,
grazing in knee-high grass, a dirty white pony.
She brings us in, shutting the casement.
The world has no mercy. We
are at the mercy of the world.

Meditation at Land's End

"Love is anterior to life,
Posterior to death,
Initial of creation and
The exponent of earth."
—Emily Dickinson

I

Tenuous firmament, the solid sand,
Expanding spits on which I stand at last,
Turn back on me as I turn toward the town.
As if in praise, a sacrifice, the world
Breaks in its chastening with excessive light
That seems to score the inside of the eye,
Autumnal broken glass across a plain
Of ocean broken into calm by land
Turning upon itself, fixed nautilus
Unfixing north from south and west to east.

II

To please their parents, children make a play,
The feast day of Saint Francis and Saint Claire
Calendric currency on which to draw
In imitation of the giving up
Of wealth and youth and self, heaping a pile
Of goods some place where goods cannot be touched.
The children feed on gazes fixed on them
And take their sweet time, too, as children will,
Until the priest bids rich and beggar kiss
And says put down the rich cap with its gem.

III

On a wood door made warm by vernal sun
A mother seeks a place to fix her case,
Which will resemble most a cicatrix.

Her abdomen is swollen with that gift,
Her legs like twigs—the yellow-green of spring.
The queen's head swivels. Imperturbable
For several hours she will fix her fate
Securely to this surface of her choice,
Dying to leave her legions on their own,
To feed on one another, live, and breed.

IV
(Nature morte)
I want to make some new thing that will live
On air and, self-substantial, move men's mouths
In praise both of the world and of release,
The peace of purple plums and of green plums
Arranged in bowls or punctuating trees
That pleases both in memory and fact,
To give fruit up in praise that stands for fruit.
Both real plums and remembered plums remain
Transfixed as molten glass, inhuman pain,
Until released by speech, a kind of food.

V
Thick schools of bluefish break beneath the pier
These last nights of warm water near the lights,
But I see only breasts that swell and turn
And hear waves rap as on an empty drum,
Some fishermen in boats that clack and groan
Illumining the body of a world
Which would be dark but for their presence there.
Another continent, another sea
First led me to a seal's bark and her gaze,
That whiskered tender gaze—insouciant, free.

VI

As thick as kiwi-seed, ringing the hold,
And in concentric circles, side by side,
Black slaves within a slaver's diagram
Reveal themselves as human when you peer
Intently at the contents of the pattern.
The slaveship Wydah foundered on near shoals,
Its gold found uncorroded. Centuries,
Drowned voices, children's, women's, men's, all lost
In the Atlantic Crossing, sweep the sea
With such laments as ringing can make praise.

VII
First Voyage
He has his slicks. His mother, back to us,
Will mend the button on his coat that hangs
Loosely on him, or on his future self,
Her dress warm red. His younger sisters see
But do not comprehend where he will go,
This twelve-year-old on his first voyage out,
A three-month's voyage or a year's, his face
A found pride tempering fear. His ears stick out,
His hair cropped short. No clapped report or shout
Can clothe him like this silence with such warmth.

Acknowledgments

I am grateful to the Phoenix Poetry Series of the University of Chicago Press for permission to reprint poems from *Iron Wheel*, *Rib Cage*, and *Watch*.

Anglican Theological Review: "Singing Schütz"
Berkeley Poetry Review: "Original Sin," "The Dresses"
Bloodroot: "Day Tripper," "Salvation," "Strasbourg"
The Chicago Review: "Magic Flute," "Prothalamion"
Cosmos: "Stroke"
Ekphrasis: "Holy Conversation"
The George Herbert Journal: from *Memoriae Matris Sacrum*
Image: "Common Ways"
Jackson Progressive: "Move On"
Millsaps Magazine: "Little Town"
Narrative: "Primal"
Open City: "Intercessor"
The Paris Review: "From the Museum"
Redlands Review: "Wake"
Scintilla: "From Fire by Fire," "King David," and "Concert to Mary,
    La Sainte Chapelle"
Sea Stories: "Wanderer"
Slate: "The Sculptor and his Muse"
Southwest Review: "The Burning of Lierpiou"
Spiritus: "Service"
La Tinaja: "Digs"
Threepenny Review: "The Harrow"
Tikkun: "Ruins," "Ark"
Verse: "Story"
Virginia Quarterly Review: "My Cousin's Son," "In the Dora Maar
    House," "Contra Artem"
Yalobusha Review: "At the Window"

Mississippi Sudan: versions of "In All Saints, Marseille," "Palm Sunday in Marseille," "From the Heights," "Capital Towers," "Protection," "Home"

I am grateful to Gladstone's Library in Hawarden, Wales, and the Dora Maar House (Houston Museum of Fine Arts) in Ménerbes, France, for residencies in the summer of 2012, to the Camargo Foundation in Cassis and the Camac Centre d'Art in Marnay-sur-Seine, France, for residencies in the springs of 2005 and 2007, the Fine Arts Work Center in Provincetown for a fellowship in 1994-1995, the Yaddo Colony in 1999 and the MacDowell Colony in 2000, as well as to the Janice C. Trimble Chair and the E. B. Stewart Chair at Millsaps College for sabbaticals, leave, and travel. And to the University of Chicago Press for publishing three books of my poems.

The translations of George Herbert are the product of a close collaboration with my friends and colleagues, Professors Emeriti of Classics Richard and Catherine Freis. I am grateful for my former colleague Claudine Chadeyras, Professor of French at Millsaps College, for comments on my Apollinaire translations.

I am grateful to Fenton Johnson, Michael Wilson, Randolph Petilos, Brian Myers, Elise and Steve Smith, Judith Page, Jim Powell, Suzanne Qualls, Alan Shapiro, Josh Weiner, Robert Pinsky, David Ferry, and Tom Sleigh; to my teachers the late Thom Gunn, Donald Davie, and Paul Alpers; to my parents, Barbara and the late David Miller; and to my husband Don Schwartz.

Notes

The Garden of Earthly Delights
> This fantastical triptych is by Hieronymus Bosch.

Jackdaws
> "nest of fierties," Scottish: roughly, "bunch of fraidy cats"

In Unity
> Brueghel the Elder and the Younger made at least three
> paintings of this scene, one now in Venice, Italy, another
> in Troyes, France, and a third in the Hermitage in Saint
> Petersburg, Russia.

From the Heights
> Jeanne Daourt's paintings are on display at the Camargo
> Foundation, Cassis, France.

Death's Triumph
> *Emathius* and *Daunia* refer to two great battles of antiquity:
> Pompey's defeat by Caesar in 48 BCE and the Romans' defeat
> by Hannibal in 216 BCE. The name "Ucalegon" (literally,
> "doesn't worry") was the first to lose his house to fire during
> the fall of Troy. *Tisiphone* was the fury who punished murder,
> *Bellona* the Roman goddess of war. *Balisters, Onagers,*
> *Scorpions,* and *Fusibalis* are all ancient, highly deadly,
> weapons of war, though nothing compared to the then newly
> invented canon. *Arviragus* was a perhaps mythical British
> king of the first century. *Orcus* was the god of the underworld
> who punished broken oaths; *Mephitis,* a Roman goddess
> of the volcano; and *Atropos,* the third and oldest of the

goddesses of fate: she who cut the thread of a life. *Cacus* was Vulcan's son, a fire-breathing giant. *Ixion* was the first man in Greek mythology to kill a member of his own family: a king, he went mad.

To the Lord

Hybla was a city in ancient Sicily famous for its sweet, flavorful honey.

Digs

While I was in residence at the Camac Centre d'Art, archeologists excavated acres to prepare the building of a plant (since cancelled) that was to process bio-fuel. I was allowed to tour the digs.

Sens

This cathedral, whose windows are here described, in Burgundy, is sometimes described as the first Gothic cathedral.

Wake

The sections describe Hurricane Katrina's aftermath for me: volunteering for the Red Cross--interviewing people about friends and family whose fates I never learned--and traveling to the badly damaged school on the Gulf Coast that would become for a few years "Camp Coast Care."

ABOUT PARACLETE PRESS

ALSO AVAILABLE IN THE PARACLETE POETRY SERIES:

Unquiet Vigil
New and Selected Poems
Brother Paul Quenon, OCSO
ISBN: 978-1-61261-560-8 | 176 pages | $21.99,
French flap paperback

What might briefly tumble through a monk's mind, or be hard chiseled over a span of years; or what quietly emerges while sitting in the dark before dawn—these are the inner and outer landscapes of the poems found in *Unquiet Vigil* collected from five decades of living a monastic life.

Endless Life
Poems of the Mystics
Scott Cairns
ISBN: 978-1-61261-520-2 | 160 pages | $18.00,
Paperback

From Saint Paul to Julian of Norwich, Scott Cairns has lovingly examined, pressed for further revelation, and set in verse the most memorable, beautiful sayings of the fathers and mothers of Christianity.

Idiot Psalms
New Poems
Scott Cairns
ISBN: 978-1-61261-515-8 | 96 pages | $17.00,
Paperback

A new collection from one of our favorite poets. Fourteen "Idiot Psalms," surrounded by dozens of other poems, make this his most challenging collection yet.